How to Look Good to an Employer

.

How to LOOK GOOD to an Employer

Rebecca Anthony
and
Gerald Roe

GLOBE FEARON

Pearson Learning Group

To Penelope in Wyoming — who never misled us — and to
Mary in Boston — who pointed the way

Illustrator: *Margaret Sanfilippo*

ISBN 0-8224-3733-3
Printed in the United States of America
  7 8 9 10   05 04 03

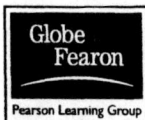

Globe
Fearon

Pearson Learning Group

1-800-321-3106
www.pearsonlearning.com

Contents

Preface   ix

1   Planning to Look Good   **1**

Your Needs: What Are the Essentials?   3
Your Interests: What Do You Enjoy?   7
Your Skills and Attributes: What Can You Offer
Employers?   8
Your Commitment: What Will You Put into It?   11
Chapter Review   12

2   Looking Good on Paper   **15**

How to Use Your Resume   15
How to Prepare Your Resume   17
Sample Resumes   22
   For Student Job Seekers   22
   For Job Seekers No Longer in School   28
Chapter Review   35

3 More Chances to Look Good on Paper — 37

An Important Form — 37
  Sample Application Forms — 38
Writing a Good Letter — 43
  Sample Business Letter Styles — 44
  Sample Letters of Application — 46
Make Forms and Letters Work for You — 52
Chapter Review — 53

4 Looking Good at Interviews — 55

Tips for Looking Good — 55
Don't Go Empty-handed — 57
Do a Little Homework — 58
  Interview Dos and Don'ts — 59
At the Interview — 63
Looking Back — 67
Follow-up Letters — 69
  Sample Follow-up Letters — 70
The Countdown — 74
The Job Offer — 74
Chapter Review — 76

5 Overcoming Obstacles — 79

If You're a Dropout — 80
If You've Been Fired — 82
If You're Handicapped — 84

If You Have a Criminal Record   87

Looking Beyond the Obstacles   89

Chapter Review   90

6   Where to Look for Jobs   93

Printed Resources   94

Employment Agencies   98

School or College Counseling/Placement Offices   101

Personnel Departments   101

Personal Contacts   102

Combining Your Resources   103

Congratulations—You're Hired   104

Chapter Review   105

Glossary   107

Appendix: Other Books of Interest   111

Index   113

Preface

Looking for a job—whether it's your first or your fifth—always creates some uneasy feelings. Even if you are confident you can get hired, there are always questions that may concern you. Will you like the new people you'll be working with? Will you still enjoy the job after you've been doing it for a while? Will there be opportunity for advancement and better pay?

Everybody wonders about such things. But these questions can only be answered by experience on the job. Therefore, it is wise not to worry about them while you are *looking* for a job. Instead, you should concentrate on the questions related to employment possibilities and getting hired.

The information in this book will help you with the questions that *can* be answered about conducting a job search. Questions such as: How do I look for a job? What is a resume? How do I write a business letter? What happens in an interview? How can I overcome certain obstacles that might be in my way? How can I get good job leads from different resources and contacts?

If you take the time to follow the advice and suggestions in this book, you will learn the answers to all these questions—and more. You will learn how to look for any kind of job—anywhere—and make yourself look good to employers while you're doing so.

The Authors

1 Planning to Look Good

Everywhere you look you can see people working, earning money, gaining experience, and enjoying their jobs. In today's world, possibilities for **employment*** are practically unlimited. Sometimes finding a job can be fairly simple. Sometimes it can take a lot of time and energy—and even a little luck. But no matter how easy or difficult your job search is, you can make it pay off if you learn to make yourself look good to employers.

Employers hire people who look good. Looking good to an employer doesn't mean you have to be the prettiest, most handsome, or best-dressed **applicant** to walk in the door. It does mean presenting yourself as a willing, dependable, honest, and capable worker who will take the job seriously.

In any job search you have several opportunities to make yourself look good to employers. This book will show you how to look good on paper and in person. It will teach you to design an effective **resume** and to write two simple letters that will help you market yourself. Understanding how to best present yourself and your qualifications at an interview will give you the edge over other job seekers.

---

* Words of special importance are printed in boldface type. These words are defined in the glossary beginning on page 107.

Looking good to employers is something you can *learn* to do. It's not a matter of discovering some hidden secret or solving a difficult puzzle. It's simply a matter of learning how to gain self-confidence and to "sell" yourself so you can impress an employer and get the job you want.

Before you start applying for jobs you must consider the following:

- your needs
- your interests
- your skills and attributes
- your commitment

Ann Slater graduated from high school last year. She is now taking two morning classes daily at a community college. Ann also is very active in a small local theater group. The group rehearses two nights a week. Ann must also be available several nights in a row every two months when the group performs its plays.

Ann lives at home with her family. But she would like to move into an apartment with her friends Jean and Pat. To do that she realizes that she will have to find a job. She knows she'll have to pay her share of the rent, utilities, and groceries. And she'll have to provide for her own transportation. All of these things will cost Ann quite a bit of money.

While in high school, Ann spent two summers as a camp counselor. She's also had many baby-sitting jobs in her neighborhood. She has had no full-time paid job experiences. But she knows that she enjoys working with people of all ages, and she feels that she can work well under pressure and can meet deadlines.

Your Needs:
What Are the Essentials?

Every job seeker has different needs. Don't make the mistake of thinking you have to follow in someone else's footsteps. What another person can do may not be possible for you because of your schedule, your **responsibilities,** or your interests. The same job isn't right for everybody.

Schedule

First think about the hours you can work. Are you looking for a full-time or part-time job? You have to know your schedule and the amount of time you can devote to a job before you can make a **commitment** to an employer.

Full-time Work   If you are looking for full-time employment, you can expect to work from 35 to 40 hours per week. Not all jobs fit into the usual Monday through Friday schedule. Some jobs require working nights and on weekends, either regularly or occasionally. You should be aware that work shifts can start at any hour of the day or night. Some employers need people to work around the clock.

Part-time Work   Are you in school? Are there other reasons you prefer not to work full-time? If so, you need to decide when your schedule will allow you to work—mornings, afternoons, evenings, or weekends. Before you can make any job decisions, you must think about the activities, studies, and responsibilities you already have to take care of. This will help you to figure out the number of hours you can devote to working at a part-time job.

Be Realistic   Don't take on more than you can handle— especially with your first job. Once you are employed, it is usually easier to *add* hours to your schedule than to ask to have your hours reduced. If you are a student, be careful about giving up your outside activities and interests unless it is financially necessary. Your only chance to take part in some of these activities is while you are in school. Being involved in activities and experiences outside the classroom can also help you look good to a future employer. Don't give up all your **recreation** just to earn a few extra dollars each week.

Income

Salary and employment **benefits** are important things to consider in any job search. What you need to earn will depend on whether or not you need to support yourself. If you're still living at home, your income needs should not be as great as if you were on your own.

In many jobs, inexperienced workers are hired at the **standard hourly minimum wage.** Other jobs may offer a fixed salary per week or month, or earnings may be based at least in part on tips, **commissions,** or **bonuses.** In addition to hourly wages or salary, some jobs include various benefits as a part of the worker's **compensation.** These benefits may include vacation time; sick leave; emergency leave; insurance plans for health care, death, or **disability;** and **retirement** programs. When looking into job possibilities, most people are also concerned with a job's earning **potential.** They want to know the amount of money they can expect to earn as a new employee. And they want to know if there are opportunities for increased earnings through **promotion** and advancement.

For some job seekers, the experience or enjoyment of a job may be more important than the take-home pay. For others, the money is **essential.** Think about your reasons for working and the amount of money you want or need to earn. Doing that will help you get a clearer focus on your job search.

Transportation

Unless you find a job within walking distance of your home, you'll have to figure out how to get to work and back again. Is it practical to use a car? Is public transportation available? What is the amount of time required to travel between work and home? The answers to these questions will also help focus your job search. Your employment choices and decisions may center around your transportation arrangements.

Clothing

Don't overlook wardrobe considerations. Your regular wardrobe might not be right for some kinds of jobs. You may have to spend money before you even take home your first paycheck. Some jobs require uniforms that you have to purchase. Even if the employer provides your work clothes, you may be responsible for keeping them presentable.

Personal Documents

In preparing for your job search, you will need to obtain certain **documents.** You should have these personal documents available for any employer who may wish to review them.

Social Security Card   Every job seeker needs a **Social Security card** and number. If you do not already have a Social Security card, go to the nearest Social Security office to apply for one. (Check your phone book for the location of the office nearest you.) It's easy to get a Social Security card, and it's free. In order to obtain one you will have to provide proof of identification.

Licenses/Certificates   Some jobs require that you be licensed to operate a motor vehicle. To operate certain types of vehicles you need to hold a chauffeur's license or a commercial driver's license. Because of state regulations, certain occupations, such as cosmetologist, emergency medical technician, and swimming instructor, require special certificates before you can be employed. Requirements may vary from one state to another. It is wise to learn beforehand if a job you're applying for requires any special documents.

References

You will want to have the names, addresses, and phone numbers of two or three people to use as **references**. They can give a possible employer information about your background and experiences. These people could be former employers, instructors, neighbors, or other people who know you well enough to recommend you to an employer. Always check with the people you plan to use as references before you give their names to employers. It's a good idea to tell them that they might receive a phone call asking for information about you.

Job Satisfaction

Steve and John are high school seniors. They have part-time jobs preparing pizzas and serving customers in a small restaurant. Steve describes his job as boring—just a way to make some money. John enjoys greeting the customers, taking their orders, and giving good service. Steve can't wait to look for another job. John hopes to work his way up to a full-time job as assistant manager.

Most workers want more from their jobs than an **income.** Finding a satisfying job can make the difference between just putting in your time or actually looking forward to going to work. Job satisfaction often depends on whether the work you do allows you to express or explore your personal interests.

Your Interests: What Do You Enjoy?

Before you look for a job, you should think about your interests. If you know the kind of work you'd enjoy doing, you'll know the kinds of jobs you'll want to explore. But be careful not to lock yourself into looking only for one particular kind of job or job setting.

The Dictionary of Occupational Titles lists thousands of different job titles. At first this may appear overwhelming. But actually, every job falls into one of three areas: working with things, working with ideas, or working with people. Most jobs combine at least two of these elements, and many will involve all three.

To help you identify your interests and the things you enjoy doing, you might ask yourself the following questions:

Do I like meeting new people? In person? On the telephone?

Do I like the challenge of persuading others to buy a new product? Or a new idea?

Do I like to work with my hands? Or my head?

Do I like working with machines? Tools? Heavy equipment?

Do I enjoy doing the same thing over and over? Or do I need a lot of variety?

Do I enjoy building or repair projects?

Do I enjoy being around people all the time? Or would I rather work alone?

Do I like traveling?

Do I feel comfortable with complicated or state-of-the-art technology?

Do I like organizing things? Checking details?

Do I like the responsibility of supervising others? Or would I rather take responsibility only for myself?

Do I enjoy the leadership role of giving instructions? Or would I rather be told what to do?

You increase your employment opportunities if you are willing to consider a variety of work settings and jobs. In many jobs, you will be able to combine more than one of your interests. And, because most jobs involve a variety of tasks, you will probably develop new interests as you gain experience.

Your Skills and Attributes: What Can You Offer Employers?

In order to get hired, you have to convince an employer that you are the right person for the job. Employers will want evidence of the skills you have acquired or developed. And they will also be interested in the personal *attributes*—or qualities—you will bring to your work.

Skills

A skill is the ability to do something fairly well. If you are looking for your first job, you may find it difficult to recognize skills you already possess. But—regardless of age, education, or previous work experience—you do have skills that can be used in any number of different jobs. Employers are looking for people with the ability to:

- speak effectively
- write clearly
- follow directions or instructions
- work cooperatively with others
- work independently
- operate equipment or machines
- lift and move heavy objects
- build or repair mechanical devices
- handle detailed activities
- collect and summarize information
- listen to others and respond appropriately
- promote a product or an idea
- think and react quickly under pressure
- motivate or persuade others
- organize projects and people

Think about your own skills compared with those listed above. This will help you to identify the things that you can do and that you can show to possible employers. Skills identification will be an important part of your job search. Many jobs will allow you to use the skills you now have. At the same time, you will develop new skills that you can take with you as your career progresses.

Attributes

Just as important as the skills you have are the qualities that make up your personality. These attributes are also of value to employers. It is important for you to be able to identify your strengths and to be able to express them.

Each job seeker has a different set of personal attributes. Use the following list to help you select the words that best describe your positive qualities:

courteous	punctual
honest	friendly
energetic	flexible
responsible	logical
cooperative	careful
trustworthy	organized
hardworking	strong
caring	sensitive
enthusiastic	patient
sensible	mature
loyal	dependable
adaptable	creative

John Cimmino is a first-time job seeker. He knows how important it is to identify his skills and attributes for possible employers. But since John hasn't had previous paid work experience, he realizes that he'll have to draw on other kinds of activities to look good to an employer.

John has spent two terms as a student government representative. He feels this shows his qualities of leadership and responsibility. John has also served as cochairman of a student fundraising drive. He was responsible for contacting local businesspeople to sponsor the school newspaper. From this job experience John learned that he likes meeting new people, the challenge of persuading others to support school projects, and exercising leadership.

John can describe himself as organized, respon-
sible, and enthusiastic. And he can support his
claims by giving examples of his experiences as a
high school student.

Your Commitment:
What Will You Put into It?

Looking for a job requires both time and effort. Even before you begin to contact employers, you should set aside time to carefully prepare for your job search. Preparation involves determining your needs and interests, identifying your skills and attributes, learning about possible employers, and learning how to present yourself well.

Be Positive

Your chances of finding a job are much better if you believe you can get one. Employers want to hire people who are pleasant and optimistic. You have to convince an employer that you have something to offer. That means presenting a confident image through every stage of your job search. Negative thinking and behavior could keep you from getting the job you want. Thinking positively will influence both the direction and the result of your job search.

Keep Trying

Looking for a job is a little like playing a game. In every game there are winners and losers. But the outcome of the game is usually not determined by chance. Steady winners are those who have a good understanding of the rules of the game and who have developed a game plan.

You have to realize that you will not get every job you apply for. There is always the possibility of being rejected.

Nobody likes rejection, but you can't be a winner every time. Disappointments are a part of nearly every job search. Don't let them get in your way. The more you play the game, the better you will get at it. And the more you play, the better your chances of winning. Don't dwell on your rejections—and don't give up. You're bound to get hired sooner or later if you keep a positive attitude.

Looking for a job is not all hard work. It can be fun. Along the way you will meet new people. You will also learn some things about yourself and about your community. Approach your job search as an adventure. Prepare for it with a sense of purpose. If you follow the advice and suggestions in the book, your adventure will be a rewarding and successful one.

Steps to Looking Good

Step One: *Identifying and understanding your needs, your interests, your skills and attributes, and making a commitment to your job search.*

Chapter Review

Your Needs

Schedule: What time commitments have I already made? What time commitments would I like to make? What hours will I be available to work?

Income: What are my expenses? What income would I *like* to have?

Transportation: How will I get to and from work? How time-consuming will my commute be?

Clothing: Is my clothing suitable for the job I would like to get? Will I need to buy clothing or to maintain clothing issued to me?

Personal   Do I have a Social Security card? Will I
Documents: need any special licenses or certificates to
                  perform my job duties?
References: Who can recommend me for a job? Have I
                  asked these people's permission to use
                  them as references? Do I have their current
                  addresses and phone numbers?

Your Interests

Do I like working with people? Or do I prefer working with things?

Your Skills and Attributes

What job skills do I have? What tasks do I perform well? What are my personal strengths?

Your Commitment

Am I motivated to find a job? Do I have a positive attitude about finding a job and about working in general?

Looking Good on Paper

When you are looking for a job, there are things that you will want an employer to know about you. Whether you want to find a part-time job, a summer job, or regular full-time employment, don't rely on an **application form** to tell your story. The best way to provide information is to prepare a resume.

A resume is a summary of your education and your achievements. It should be short and easy to read. Your resume should tell an employer your name, your address, and your telephone number. It should also list information about your educational background, including any diplomas, degrees, or certificates you have earned. And your resume should tell what you have done or are presently doing, and what your interests and skills are. Think of your resume as a picture of you. It may not show what you look like. But it will help an employer form an image of you.

How to Use Your Resume

Knowing when and how to use your resume will give you confidence as you begin your job search. A resume may be used at different times and for different purposes. You can give an employer a resume in three different ways:

With Application Forms   If you are applying for a job in person, attach a copy of your resume to the completed application form provided by the employer.

With a Cover Letter In response to a job announcement in the newspaper, you can send your resume along with a letter of application.

At Interviews Always give a copy of your resume to the interviewer either at the beginning or at the end of the interview.

Don't be hesitant about giving your resume to employers. They will appreciate having the information. And they will be impressed that you have thought about what you have done and organized the information on paper. An employer's task of hiring **qualified** people is made easier if the job seeker provides an organized, accurate resume.

Employers are not the only people who find your resume helpful. You can give copies to people who have knowledge of your abilities and experiences. These might include instructors, former or current employers, supervisors, and neighbors. Your resume will help these people give current and accurate information about you when they are asked to comment on your background.

Don't Be Shy

A good resume is an honest, factual account of what you have done. You might even think of it as a "brag-sheet." When you write your resume be sure to include your achievements and your activities. Always be positive and emphasize your strong points. You should not exaggerate or lie on your resume, but you shouldn't downplay what you have to offer, either.

Don't tell more than is necessary. Your resume is not your autobiography. Concentrate on presenting information that can help you get a job.

Cory Berwald wants to find a summer job. Although he has no particular job in mind, he knows that he wants to work outdoors. In his community there are employers in construction, landscaping, and road repair. In any of these fields, physical strength is a plus. So Cory's resume will emphasize activities that show he has the ability to lift and move heavy objects. He has lifted weights at the local YMCA for the past three years, and he participated in a recent boxing tournament. Even though he didn't win his bout, the fact that he participated is evidence of his physical fitness.

How to Prepare Your Resume

There are no secrets to writing a good resume, and there aren't any magic formulas. But there are ten rules that can help take the mystery out of what a good resume should look like.

1. Make It Easy to Read A good resume is short and to the point. It is easier to read short sentences or phrases than long paragraphs. The reader should be able to scan your resume in just a few seconds.

2. Make It Relevant Employers need to know about your qualifications for a job. They don't need to know your age, height, weight, color of eyes and hair, race, religion, marital status, or number of **dependents.** Federal and state guidelines forbid employers from requesting this information before hiring someone. There is no reason for you to volunteer it on your resume.

3. Make the Content Specific Include only those activities and experiences related to your immediate goal. Be sure to list the achievements that clearly show your qualifications for the job you seek. If you are considering very different types of jobs, you might prepare separate resumes to emphasize different accomplishments and skills.

4. Emphasize Strong Points Write about the things you have done, not about things you want to do. Never point out weaknesses. Tell the employer what you're good at.

5. Tell the Truth Be accurate. Employers *do* check up on you. If they learn that you haven't been truthful, they won't want to hire you.

6. Make It Look Good Design your resume so that it is easy to read. You don't need fancy **graphics** or special lettering to make your resume stand out. Don't crowd it. Leave plenty of white space, and balance the type on the page.

7. Avoid Errors Check your spelling carefully. Make sure you are using the correct words to describe your activities. Type carefully and correct any errors neatly. Read it over to be sure that no mistakes have been made.

8. Get a Second Opinion Ask someone whose opinion you respect to review your resume. In this way you can learn if it creates a positive image of you. That person might also be able to make some recommendations that could improve the resume's content or appearance.

9. Make Copies Resumes should be typed, but don't try to make an original for each application. Copies can be made from a perfectly typed original. Resumes can also be produced on personal computers, or they may be typeset at a print shop. Use standard size (8½″ × 11″) paper of good quality.

10. Be Neat The resume you give to employers should be crisp and clean. Be careful not to smudge, crease, or stain your paper. If you must fold your resume to fit it into an envelope, be sure to fold it carefully.

Use Action Words

A resume must be interesting to read. Carefully select the words to describe your experiences and accomplishments, so that an employer will want to read the entire resume. The following action words, or others like them, can help your resume come alive.

elected	initiated
performed	earned
delivered	chosen
collected	won
nominated	built
selected	designed
directed	learned
worked	mastered
produced	volunteered
participated	encouraged
represented	trained
organized	sold
operated	completed
developed	assisted

Write Action Phrases

Look at the list of action words and think of how you could use them on your resume. Don't limit yourself to things that you have done in school or on other jobs. Think about your activities at home and in the community as well. You may be surprised at how many things you have accomplished. You can share these accomplishments with an employer by using these action words in phrases that describe your experiences. Keep your phrases short, clear, and simple. Action phrases should communicate information at a glance.

> *College student April Williams has worked to support herself while in school and has also participated in a number of activities. Her action phrases might read:*
>> *EARNED 100% of education expenses*
>> *NOMINATED as class representative for student government*
>> *PERFORMED featured or lead roles in three plays*
>> *PARTICIPATED in community chorus for two years*
>
> *High school student Scott Crawford used these action phrases to tell possible employers about his accomplishments and responsibilities:*
>> *MANAGED football concession stand*
>> *SUPERVISED three volunteers*
>> *BUILT a bookcase that was used as a model for evening classes*
>> *DESIGNED and supervised construction of parade floats*

Choosing Resume Headings

Once you have thought about your activities and accomplishments, you need to think about organizing this material on your resume. In order to make your resume clear and easy to read, you should divide it into several sections. Each section tells something important about you. Not everyone will use the same headings. Each resume will be different because each person has a different story to tell. Look at the list of section headings below and select those you would like to use.

SCHOOLS ATTENDED

EDUCATION

EDUCATIONAL PREPARATION

EMPLOYMENT

PART-TIME WORK

SUMMER WORK EXPERIENCES

VOLUNTEER EXPERIENCES

RELATED EXPERIENCES

SPECIAL SKILLS

PERSONAL ATTRIBUTES

COMPETENCIES

ACHIEVEMENTS

ACCOMPLISHMENTS

ACTIVITIES

HONORS AND AWARDS

SPECIAL HONORS

COMMUNITY SERVICES

LEISURE ACTIVITIES

INTERESTS

CAREER HIGHLIGHTS

COURSES OF INTEREST

SCHOOL HIGHLIGHTS

Sample Resumes

Take a look at the sample resumes on the next several pages. Notice how the information is organized, and watch for action words and phrases. You might want to combine features from several of the samples to create a resume that tells your story and makes you look good to employers.

Resumes for Student Job Seekers

> Part-time Jobs
>
> Summer Jobs
>
> College Internships

Look For:

> Style
>
> Layout
>
> Organization
>
> Action Words and Phrases
>
> Activities and Interests
>
> Educational Background

JESSE ROBINSON HODGES

2A Cypress Lane
Atlanta, Georgia   30303
(404) 658-8965

EDUCATIONAL PREPARATION	Strawberry Point High School 1986-Present Atlanta, Georgia
SCHOOL ACTIVITIES	Mu Alpha Theta, Mathematics Club Sophomore Singers Student Senate Member and Volunteer Service, Committee Chairperson

COURSE
HIGHLIGHTS

European History   Biology
Computer Science   French
Geometry   Contemporary Scene

HONORS
& AWARDS

State Finalist, History Day Competition
Member, Boy's Quartet, State I Rating
Community Service Award, Boy Scouts of
  America
Honor Roll, Four semesters
Member, Honor Society

REFERENCES PROVIDED UPON REQUEST

VERONICA ALLEN

918 Maggard Street
Rockford, Illinois 61121
(815) 338-5368

--------SCHOOLS ATTENDED--------

| North High School | Madison, Wisconsin | 1984-86 |
| Rockford City High | Rockford, Illinois | 1986-88 |

(will graduate May 26, 1988)

--------ACCOMPLISHMENTS--------

MANAGER of varsity softball teams in Madison and Rockford

RANKED number one chess player at Midwest regional games

ELECTED class treasurer junior year

HOST for senior citizens at the Aging and Youth Conference held at
Rockford City High

--------PART-TIME WORK--------

City Star Daily News Madison, Wisconsin	Carrier	4 years
Rockyview Stables Rockford, Illinois	Trail Guide and Horse Care	2 summers
Pizza Hut Rockford, Illinois	Dish Washer & Cook	currently employed

--------LEISURE INTERESTS--------

horseback riding	fishing
ceramics	experimental cooking
computer games	painting
chess	spectator sports

--------REFERENCES--------

Jerry W. Jensen	Head softball coach 356-7562	Rockford City High
Sandra Lynn	Supervisor 298-8674	City Star Daily News
Jane McCormick	Owner 386-7000	Rockyview Stables
Jim Allen	Manager 356-9632	Pizza Hut

BLAINE C. MILLER

1333 Regal Street
Davenport, Iowa 52604
833-4734

WORK EXPERIENCE

June, 1985 - present

Hy-Vee Grocery Store, Rochester Avenue, Davenport, Iowa
Stock shelves, carry-out, and customer service

June, 1980 - August, 1983

Davenport Daily News, Davenport, Iowa
Paper delivery to 60 subscribers

SCHOOL & COMMUNITY ACTIVITIES

Journalism

Photography Editor, Student Yearbook, 1985-1987
Photographer, Student Newspaper, 1984-1986

Athletics

Manager, Varsity Football Team, 1984, 1985
Manager, Varsity Basketball Team, 1985, 1986

Elected Offices

Class Treasurer, 1984-1985
Class Vice-President, 1985-1986

Scouting

Six years in Troop 212
Eagle Scout, 1984
Assistant troop leader, 1985-1987

Church

Assist with programs and retreats for high school students

EDUCATION

September, 1984 - present

Regina High School, Davenport, Iowa

REFERENCES

References will be furnished upon request

RESUME OF: CHRISTINA LOPOS

ADDRESS: 28 Eastwood Drive
                 Iowa City, Iowa 52240
                 (319) 357-2772

PERSONAL ATTRIBUTES: energetic   responsible   cooperative
                      courteous   trustworthy   hard-working
                      flexible   organized   careful

EDUCATION: City High School, Iowa City, Iowa
                 Diploma: 1988

COURSES OF INTEREST: Business Math
                      Typing   Computer I
                      World History   Auto Mechanics
                      Contemporary Problems   Family Living and
                                          Social Relationships

EMPLOYMENT: Cashier, Younkers Department Store, Iowa City, Iowa
                 1987 - present, weekends

                 Station Attendant, Tom's Quick Fill, Iowa City, Iowa
                 1985 - 1986, part-time and vacations

                 Child care, baby-sitting in Iowa City homes
                 1984 - present

ACHIEVEMENTS: City High Volleyball, lettered in 1985 & 1986
                 Homecoming Committee, 1984

COMMUNITY ACTIVITIES: Volunteer, Iowa City Pals Program
                       Softball Coach, Iowa City Parks and Recreation

REFERENCES: Mary Tale, Supervisor at Younkers, 351-7876

                 Tom Binkard, Owner of Tom's Quick Fill, 338-9024

                 George Smarts, City High teacher, 351-4552

DAVID M. CHARLES
4100 Lake Breeze Avenue North
Brooklyn Center, Minnesota 55427
(612) 537-3742

OBJECTIVE

Summer internship in marketing research

EDUCATION

University of Minnesota - Twin Cities, 1984 - present

Business major, emphasis in marketing
130 quarter hours completed as of June, 1987
Anticipated graduation date June, 1988
Grade point average: 3.89/4.00 (business courses)
3.72/4.00 (overall)

Brooklyn Center Senior High School, 1981-1984

College preparatory course
Grade point average: 3.86/4.00

ACTIVITIES AND HONORS

Elected to represent College of Business in the University
of Minnesota, Student Senate, 1986

Volunteer, 6th District Congressional campaign, 1986
Assisted with coordination of telephone campaign and
door-to-door surveys

Chamber of Commerce Scholarship, 1984

Student Council President, 1983-1984

Selected representative to Minnesota Boys' State, 1983

Nominated for Youth for Understanding study award, 1983

Junior Class President, 1982-1983

WORK EXPERIENCE

Minnesota Student Union Catering Service, 1984-1987
Contributed to college expenses by working as waiter
and bartender

Dayton's Department Store, Brookdale Mall, 1983-1984
Stock clerk in sporting goods and show departments

REFERENCES

Available upon request

Resumes for Job Seekers No Longer in School
> Full-time Employment
> Job Change
> Career Advancement

Look For:
> Style
> Layout
> Organization
> Action Words and Phrases
> Skills and Interests
> Description of Duties
> Employment History

NATALIE N. WU

28 Royal Drive
McAllen, Texas 78501
(512) 423-5232

JOB OBJECTIVE_____

Retail Management

ACCOMPLISHMENTS_____

Managed all aspects of business operation
Selected merchandise for retail
Supervised staff including sales clerks, bookkeeper & custodian
Maintained inventory
Increased sales by 25%

COMPETENCIES_____

Training   Public relations
Supervising   Budget & cost analysis
Marketing   Staff management

EXPERIENCE_____

Manager   The Fashion Store   McAllen, Texas
                  1985 to present

Clerk   Neiman Marcus   Dallas, Texas
                  1982 to 1985

TRAINING_____

Internship   Carson, Pirie, Scott & Co.   Chicago, Illinois
                  Fall, 1981

Coursework   Stephens College   Columbia, Missouri
                  1980 to 1982

Diploma   Dallas Academy   Dallas, Texas
                  1976 to 1980

PERSONAL INTERESTS_____

Fashion design   Modeling   Quilt making   Tennis

REFERENCES_____

John Lopos   Distric Manager   (512) 426-2008
                  The Fashion Store

Joan Wesley   Floor Supervisor   (214) 824-3020
                  Neiman Marcus

LAUREL ANN ZIMMERMAN

503 Fourth Street, S.E.
Medford, Oregon 97501
(503) 776-5339

QUALIFICATIONS: Computer Skills including information and
word processing systems

Typing, 80 words per minute

Gregg shorthand, 120 words per minute

Familiarity with calculator, copy machines,
postage meter, and various filing systems.

Experience with answering telephones, taking
messages, and greeting visitors

EDUCATION: Grants Pass Community College
Grants Pass, Oregon
Completed one-year course in secretarial studies,
July, 1987

Course highlights: Information Systems
Word Processing
Computer Programming
Introductory Accounting
Office Procedures

Medford Senior High School
Medford, Oregon
Diploma, June, 1986

EXPERIENCE: Work-study position in Registrar's Office,
Grants Pass Community College, 1986-1987

Duties included retrieving, copying,
and mailing transcripts; filing, and
assisting full-time staff as required

Student assistant in Principal's office,
Medford Senior High School, 1985-1986

Duties included answering telephone,
miscellaneous typing, back-up for
receptionist

REFERENCES: Available upon request

MARIA LOPEZ

1004 Madison Avenue

Santa Barbara, California 93108

(805) 969-5515

SKILLS

Basic Computer Applications
Word Processing Techniques
General Supervision
Speaking & Public Relations

EMPLOYMENT HISTORY

Library Clerk, Public Library, Goleta, California   1986 - present

Responsibilities included assisting patrons with questions regarding
video and audio equipment; processing fines for overdue materials;
reading for children story hours.

Teacher's Aide, Seaside School, Santa Barbara, California 1983 - 1985 (summers)

Responsibilities included assisting head primary teacher; supervising
free play and lunchroom; designing bulletin boards; organizing and
directing a school-wide play.

EDUCATION

Goleta Public High School   Diploma, 1985
Goleta, California

Oceanfront Community Education Center   Evening Courses, 1985 -
Montecito, California

RECENT COURSES

Introduction to Operating the Apple Computer
Dynamics of Effective Supervision
Sales Success: A Workshop for Women
Spanish 1

CIVIC ACTIVITIES

Member, County Historic Preservation Committee
Volunteer, Hospital Guild Gift Shop
Planner, Santa Barbara Crafts & Arts Celebration

REFERENCES

Available Upon Request

JOHN STUART WARREN

739 Sycamore Street
Oklahoma City, Oklahoma 73102
405/525/7789

PROFESSIONAL EXPERIENCE

Emergency Room Staff Nurse, Part-time
Foster Community Hospital
Houston, Texas
1986-1987

RELATED EXPERIENCE

Orderly, Orthopedics & Oncology Wards
Mercy Hospital
Enid, Oklahoma
1981-1983

LICENSE

Licensed as Registered Nurse
Oklahoma and Texas

EDUCATION

Recent Continuing Education Courses
include:

    Psychology of Eating Disorders
    Emergency Treatment for Burns
    Prevention of Trauma for Athletes
    Treatment of Juvenile Diabetes
    Hospice Care

Mercy Hospital Nursing School
Enid, Oklahoma
Three-year diploma program
1983-1986

Meridian High School
Meridian, Oklahoma
College preparatory program
1978-1981

COMMUNITY ACTIVITIES

Assistant Coach, Babe Ruth Baseball
Enid Parks Bike Path Committee
  (charter member)
Project Green Volunteer
Member, Sierra Club

REFERENCES

Will be furnished upon request

JAMES ARNOLD

1624 Dorset Avenue
Newton Centre, Massachusetts 02163
(617) 329-3920

AUTO MECHANIC

Three years experience in repair shop and new car dealership

Repaired and maintained General Motors and Mazda automobiles
at new car dealerships

Experience in power train overhaul, gas and diesel engine tune-up
and repair

Certified Auto Mechanic
Certified Mazda Automobile Mechanic
Buick Craftsman League: General Motors

EMPLOYMENT HISTORY

Buick/Mazda Village, Newton Centre, Massachusetts, 1983-1986

Kendall Mobil Service Station, Springfield, Massachusetts, 1982-1983

Ken's Auto Service, Turner's Falls, Massachusetts, 1978-1981

EDUCATION

Springfield Technical Community College, Springfield, Massachusetts
Associate's degree, Automotive Technologies, 1983
G.E.D., 1981

REFERENCES

Glenn Nelson, General Manager, Buick/Mazda Village (617) 329-0437

Thomas Nagel, Service Manager, Buick/Mazda Village (617) 329-0439

Ken Harris, Owner, Ken's Auto Service (413) 831-3368

The Final Product

Now you've looked at the sample resumes. You've experimented with different headings, layouts, and phrases. After you come up with a good draft of your resume, put it away for a day or two. When you come back to it, you might see some items that need to be revised. Once you feel satisfied with the content, the next step is choosing a production method.

Depending on how much time you have and how much money you can spend, there are three ways of producing the resume: reproductions from a typed original, printing from a computer, and professional typesetting. Whichever method you choose, the final product should be on good quality paper. Gimmicks such as bright colors, odd typefaces, and lighthearted graphics should be avoided. Although they may make your resume stand out, it will be for the wrong reasons.

But It's Not Really Final

The first resume you prepare is just the beginning. As you gain experience, and as your interests change, so will your resume. In order to continue to look good to employers, you will need to update your resume from time to time. Adding experiences, activities, and new skills as you acquire them is the way you show employers that you are growing professionally. You will also need to remove outdated items and those that become less important. Never update your resume by penciling in new information or crossing out outdated items. Prepare a new original whenever you make any changes. Be sure to keep a copy of each version of your resume. Updating it will then be easier when you need it for your next job search.

Steps to Looking Good

Step One: Identifying and understanding your needs, your interests, your skills and attributes, and making a commitment to your job search.

Step Two: *Knowing how to prepare a resume and understanding how to use it.*

Chapter Review

Using Your Resume

Employers: Why do employers want a resume? How can I present my resume to an employer?

References: How will my resume help people recommend me for jobs?

What's in a Resume?

What do I need to tell an employer? Won't it look like I'm bragging? What are the rules for writing resumes? How can I make my resume interesting to read? Do the words I use tell my story? How can I organize my resume? Should all resumes look alike? Do I need more than one resume?

Resume Production

Can I make copies of my resume? Which production method should I use? Do unusual resumes give job seekers an edge?

Updating

Will I only use my resume for my first job? Why do resumes need to be updated?

3) More Chances to Look Good on Paper

Nearly every job seeker says that filling out application forms is the least interesting part of the job search. And it's true—this will probably never be one of your favorite activities. However, businesses of all kinds and sizes often require all job seekers to complete an application form. Employers find it more convenient to obtain information on a standard form that everyone fills out. Therefore, it's important to realize how these forms are used so that you do a good job of completing them.

An Important Form

Do not be misled by the appearance of the application form. Some organizations use a slick professional package. Others use a short photocopied form. Whichever kind you're given, you should treat it seriously. Not all forms look alike, but they all have the same purpose. They all seek to obtain information about each applicant's qualifications and previous experiences.

Many employers use the applications as the first step in the hiring process. Even the simplest application form may be used as a screening device. Sloppy, hard-to-read, incomplete applications can hurt your chances for the job. Regardless of what the form looks like, do your best to complete it neatly and accurately. Sometimes this can be difficult. You may be in a room crowded with other job seekers, standing at a busy counter, or trying to write using your knee as a desk. Do your best under whatever circumstances you're in.

Like your resume, the application form creates an image of you. In order to make the most favorable impression, complete it very carefully. Be sure to follow all instructions. You won't want to make any mistakes or skip any items. Do not leave blanks. If any section of the form does not apply to you, put a dash (—) or the letters N/A (not applicable) in that space. By doing this, you let the employer know that you have read every question.

Take a Second Look

Looking good on the application form is an important step in getting hired. Before handing in your application, check to make sure that you have:

- included your full name and address
- answered every question
- spelled every word correctly
- corrected any mistakes neatly

Always attach a copy of your resume to the completed application form. The resume can provide more information about you and may include items which do not appear on the employer's form. You can also use your resume to refer to as you fill in the blanks on the form.

Sample Application Forms

Whatever the application form looks like, it will probably ask for the same kind of information requested on the following samples.

B. Dalton
BOOKSELLER

APPLICATION FOR EMPLOYMENT
An Equal Opportunity Employer

PERSONAL DATA

NAME LAST	FIRST	MIDDLE	DATE

PRESENT ADDRESS   (STREET, CITY, STATE, ZIP CODE)

PERMANENT ADDRESS   (IF DIFFERENT FROM ABOVE)

HOME PHONE	BUSINESS PHONE	SOCIAL SECURITY NUMBER	ARE YOU 16 OR OVER
			YES ____ NO ____

ARE YOU A U.S. CITIZEN?
YES ____ NO ____
IF NOT A U.S. CITIZEN LIST VISA NUMBER & EXPIRATION DATE
NUMBER _____ DATE ____

HAVE YOU EVER BEEN CONVICTED OF A CRIME? (A CONVICTION WILL NOT BE AN ABSOLUTE BAR TO AN OFFER OF EMPLOYMENT.) YES ____ NO ____
IF YES, EXPLAIN _____

TRAX

PLACEMENT INFORMATION

POSITION OR TYPE OF WORK DESIRED

ARE YOU INTERESTED IN
____ FULL TIME   ____ PART TIME   ____ PERM.   ____ TEMP.

	SUNDAY	MONDAY	TUESDAY	WEDNESDAY	THURSDAY	FRIDAY	SATURDAY
HOURS AVAILABLE TO WORK AM							
PM							

SALARY OR WAGE DESIRED	DATE AVAILABLE	WHO OR WHAT REFERRED YOU TO B. DALTON?

HAVE YOU EVER BEEN EMPLOYED BY B. DALTON (OR ANY OPERATING COMPANY OF DAYTON HUDSON CORPORATION) BEFORE?
YES ____ NO ____ IF YES, WHEN & WHERE ____

FOR OFFICE POSITION ONLY:
DO YOU TYPE: YES ____ NO ____ WPM ____ TAKE DICTATION YES ____ NO ____ WPM ____
OFFICE MACHINES YOU OPERATE _____

EDUCATION RECORD

LIST LAST HIGH SCHOOL AND ALL BUSINESS, TRADE SCHOOLS AND COLLEGES ATTENDED

NAME AND LOCATION OF SCHOOL	DATES ATTENDED	MAJOR/ MINOR	DEGREE	CUMULATIVE AVERAGE

EXTRACURRICULAR ACTIVITIES (INCLUDE OFFICES HELD, SCHOLARSHIPS, AWARDS, HONORS, SPORTS, ETC.) YOU ARE NOT REQUIRED TO LIST ACTIVITIES WHICH MAY REVEAL YOUR RACE, RELIGION, SEX, OR NATIONAL ORIGIN.

B. DALTON BOOKSELLER DOES NOT DISCRIMINATE IN HIRING OR TERMS OR CONDITIONS OF EMPLOYMENT ON THE BASIS OF RACE, COLOR, CREED, RELIGION, SEX, NATIONAL ORIGIN, AGE, OR ANY OTHER BASIS UPON WHICH DISCRIMINATION IS PROHIBITED BY THE MUNICIPAL, STATE, OR FEDERAL LAW. NO QUESTION ON THIS APPLICATION IS INTENDED TO SECURE INFORMATION TO BE USED FOR SUCH DISCRIMINATION.

Form No 60004 (2/83)

17313 – bann division, stuart-hooper co., mn

EMPLOYMENT HISTORY

LIST ALL EMPLOYERS WITH CURRENT OR MOST RECENT EMPLOYMENT FIRST. LEAVE NO TIME UNACCOUNTED FOR. INCLUDE MILITARY SERVICE. IF LIMITED PREVIOUS EMPLOYMENT, LIST THREE PERSONS, NOT RELATED, WHO HAVE KNOWN YOU FOR SOME TIME.

PRESENT LAST EMPLOYER		
	TELEPHONE NUMBER ( )	SUPERVISOR'S NAME
ADDRESS		
	DATES EMPLOYED	BASE SALARY OR WAGE
POSITION TITLE	/ TO / MO. YR. MO. YR.	START
SUMMARY OF DUTIES		CURRENT OR END
		DATE OF LAST INCREASE
REASON FOR LEAVING OR SEEKING CHANGE OF POSITION		

FIRST PREVIOUS EMPLOYER		
	TELEPHONE NUMBER ( )	SUPERVISOR'S NAME
ADDRESS		
	DATES EMPLOYED	BASE SALARY OR WAGE
POSITION TITLE	/ TO / MO. YR. MO. YR.	START
SUMMARY OF DUTIES		CURRENT OR END
		DATE OF LAST INCREASE
REASON FOR LEAVING OR SEEKING CHANGE OF POSITION		

NEXT PREVIOUS EMPLOYER		
	TELEPHONE NUMBER ( )	SUPERVISOR'S NAME
ADDRESS		
	DATES EMPLOYED	BASE SALARY OR WAGE
POSITION TITLE	/ TO / MO. YR. MO. YR.	START
SUMMARY OF DUTIES		CURRENT OR END
		DATE OF LAST INCREASE
REASON FOR LEAVING OR SEEKING CHANGE OF POSITION		

MAY WE CONTACT YOUR CURRENT EMPLOYER   YES _____   NO _____   PHONE ( ) _____

OCCUPATIONAL REFERENCES

(LIST PERSONAL REFERENCES ONLY IF YOU HAVE NO OCCUPATIONAL REFERENCES)

CHECK ONE ___ OCCUPATIONAL REF. ___ PERSONAL REFERENCE	NAME	OCCUPATION	
			YEARS ACQUAINTED
ADDRESS (STREET, CITY, STATE, ZIP CODE)			TELEPHONE NUMBER ( )
CHECK ONE ___ OCCUPATIONAL REF. ___ PERSONAL REFERENCE	NAME	OCCUPATION	
			YEARS ACQUAINTED
ADDRESS (STREET, CITY, STATE, ZIP CODE)			TELEPHONE NUMBER ( )

IN ORDER FOR B. DALTON TO CONDUCT REFERENCE CHECKS PLEASE, LIST HERE OTHER NAMES YOU HAVE WORKED UNDER _____

HEALTH INFORMATION

DO YOU HAVE ANY HEALTH RESTRICTIONS WHICH WOULD INTERFERE WITH YOUR ABILITY TO PERFORM THE WORK FOR WHICH YOU ARE APPLYING   YES _____   NO _____ . IF YES, DESCRIBE _____

IMPORTANT, READ BEFORE SIGNING

The filing of an application with B. Dalton is a preliminary step to employment. It does not obligate B. Dalton to offer employment, or the applicant to accept employment. An offer of employment, if made, is for employment at will and is not to be construed as a guarantee of continued employment. B. Dalton reserves the right to terminate the employment of any employee at any time. Any employee also has the right to terminate his or her employment with B. Dalton at any time.

• NOTICE TO APPLICANTS AS REQUIRED BY THE FAIR CREDIT REPORTING ACT
As part of our employment process, an investigative consumer report may be prepared regarding an applicant's character, general reputation, personal characteristics, and mode of living. Additional information as to the nature and scope of such a report, if made, will be provided upon the applicant's written request.

• I authorize investigation of all matters contained in this application which B. Dalton may deem relevant to my employment and authorize my previous employers or other persons having information concerning me or my record to report such information to B. Dalton and such persons are hereby released from all liability for issuing such information. B. Dalton will keep all such information confidential except where such information is required to be released by law or order of a court or other authority. I understand and agree that I will be subject to immediate dismissal if it is subsequently discovered that the information herein is untrue or that I have failed to disclose a material fact. I understand that if employed by B. Dalton, such employment will occur at will and no contract of employment, express or implied, is created and that no representative of B. Dalton has any authority to enter into any agreement for employment of any specified period of time, or to make any agreement contrary to the foregoing. I understand that if I receive an offer of employment and I accept the position, I will be required to complete additional information necessary for company record keeping requirements.

SIGNATURE

DATE

Wendy's OLD FASHIONED HAMBURGERS

EXEMPT EMPLOYMENT APPLICATION
WE ARE AN EQUAL OPPORTUNITY EMPLOYER
MALE/FEMALE

Wendy's OLD FASHIONED HAMBURGERS

P.O. Box 256
4288 W. Dublin Granville Rd.
Dublin, Ohio 43017

VARIOUS FEDERAL, STATE AND LOCAL LAWS PROHIBIT DISCRIMINATION BASED ON RACE, COLOR, SEX, RELIGION, NATIONAL ORIGIN, ANCESTRY, AGE (AS PRESCRIBED BY LAW) HANDICAP OR MARITAL STATUS. WENDY'S IS AN EQUAL OPPORTUNITY EMPLOYER AND YOUR RESPONSE TO ANY QUESTION WILL NOT BE USED AS A BASIS FOR DISCRIMINATION BUT WILL BE JUDGED ON IT'S RELEVANCE TO THE POSITION YOU ARE SEEKING.

NAME (LAST)	(FIRST)		(MIDDLE)	SOCIAL SECURITY NO.

HOME ADDRESS	CITY	STATE	ZIP CODE	AREA CODE HOME TELEPHONE NO.

NAME OF PERSON TO NOTIFY IN EMERGENCY	ADDRESS	CITY	STATE	TELEPHONE

POSITION APPLIED FOR	DATE AVAILABLE

WILL YOU RELOCATE	WHAT % OF TIME WILL YOU TRAVEL %	GEOGRAPHICAL PREFERENCE	HOW DID YOU COME IN CONTACT WITH WENDY'S?

WITHIN THE LAST 5 YRS. HAVE YOU EVER BEEN CONVICTED OF A FELONY? ☐ NO ☐ YES	IF YES GIVE DETAILS ON BACK PAGE	HAVE YOU EVER WORKED FOR OR APPLIED FOR A POSITION WITH WENDY'S? IF YES GIVE DETAILS ON BACK PAGE

EDUCATION	INSTITUTION NAME & ADDRESS	DID YOU GRADUATE?	MAJOR FIELD OF STUDY	CLASS STANDING
HIGH SCHOOL				
		DEGREE REC'D		
COLLEGE OR UNIVERSITY				
		DEGREE REC'D		
GRADUATE STUDY				
		DEGREE REC'D		
OTHER				
		DEGREE REC'D		

PERSONAL REFERENCES: LIST FORMER EMPLOYERS

NAME	ADDRESS	PHONE	OCCUPATION	YEARS KNOWN

WENDY'S ER-1 (4/77)

CONTINUED ON BACK PAGE

EMPLOYMENT RECORD

PLEASE LIST ALL EMPLOYMENT STARTING WITH MOST RECENT ACCOUNT FOR ALL PERIODS (INCLUDING U.S. ARMED FORCES, PERIODS OF UNEMPLOYMENT AND VOLUNTARY SERVICES.)

LIST YOUR MOST RECENT POSITION HELD:

MAY WE CONTACT YOUR PRESENT EMPLOYER? ☐ YES ☐ NO

EMPLOYER'S NAME AND COMPLETE ADDRESS /PHONE	DATES EMPLOYED		POSITION TITLE
	FROM	TO	
			NAME OF TITLE OF SUPERVISOR
	SALARY		
	START	FINAL	REASON FOR LEAVING
EMPLOYER'S NAME AND COMPLETE ADDRESS /PHONE	DATES EMPLOYED		POSITION TITLE
	FROM	TO	
			NAME AND TITLE OF SUPERVISOR
	SALARY		
	START	FINAL	REASON FOR LEAVING
EMPLOYER'S NAME AND COMPLETE ADDRESS /PHONE	DATES EMPLOYED		POSITION TITLE
	FROM	TO	
			NAME AND TITLE OF SUPERVISOR
	SALARY		
	START	FINAL	REASON FOR LEAVING
EMPLOYER'S NAME AND COMPLETE ADDRESS /PHONE	DATES EMPLOYED		POSITION TITLE
	FROM	TO	
			NAME AND TITLE OF SUPERVISOR
	SALARY		
	START	FINAL	REASON FOR LEAVING
EMPLOYER'S NAME AND COMPLETE ADDRESS /PHONE	DATES EMPLOYED		POSITION TITLE
	FROM	TO	
			NAME AND TITLE OF SUPERVISOR
	SALARY		
	START	FINAL	REASON FOR LEAVING

ADDITIONAL INFORMATION

FOR EMPLOYEE RELATION USE ONLY

EMPLOYEES WILL BE ENGAGED, SUBJECT TO RECEIPT OF SATISFACTORY REFERENCES. IN MAKING THIS APPLICATION FOR EMPLOYMENT IT IS UNDERSTOOD THAT AN INVESTIGATION MAY BE MADE WHEREBY INFORMATION IS OBTAINED THROUGH PERSONAL INTERVIEWS WITH NEIGHBORS, FRIENDS OR OTHERS WITH WHOM YOU ARE ACQUAINTED. THE INQUIRY INCLUDES INFORMATION AS TO YOUR CHARACTER, GENERAL REPUTATION, PERSONAL CHARACTERISTICS AND MODE OF LIVING, IF RELATED TO THE JOB FOR WHICH YOU ARE APPLYING. YOU HAVE THE RIGHT TO MAKE A WRITTEN REQUEST WITHIN A REASONABLE PERIOD OF TIME TO RECEIVE ADDITIONAL, DETAILED INFORMATION ABOUT THE NATURE AND SCOPE OF THIS INVESTIGATION. FALSIFICATION. IT IS UNDERSTOOD THAT ANY FALSE STATEMENT IN THIS APPLICATION IS SUFFICIENT CAUSE FOR DISMISSAL.

APPLICANT'S SIGNATURE   DATE SIGNED

WE APPRECIATE YOUR TIME AND CONSIDERING WENDY'S FOR POSSIBLE EMPLOYMENT

Writing a Good Letter

Denise Karamanis got her first job at the Busy Bee Grocery without even applying for it. Denise's older sister had worked for the owners, and when she moved away Denise just stepped into the job. Now that Denise is graduating from high school, she is looking for a full-time job. So, although she has never done it before, Denise needs to write a letter of application.

Business letters are different from the letters you write to friends or relatives. First of all, business letters look different. They should always be written on standard size paper (8½" × 11"). Never use postcards, notepads, or decorated stationery. If at all possible, you should type your own letters. If you can't type, consider asking or hiring someone else to type your letters for you. Handwritten letters should be sent only as a last resort. If this is your only choice, write the letter using a blue or black pen. Be sure to use your best handwriting or printing.

Business letters contain some parts that are not usually included in personal correspondence. The parts of a business letter are:

- return address
- date
- inside address
- greeting
- body
- closing
- signature
- writer's name, typed or printed
- enclosure notation (used only when one or more items accompany the letter)

Sample Business Letter Styles

The following samples show how the various parts of a business letter are arranged in two standard business styles.

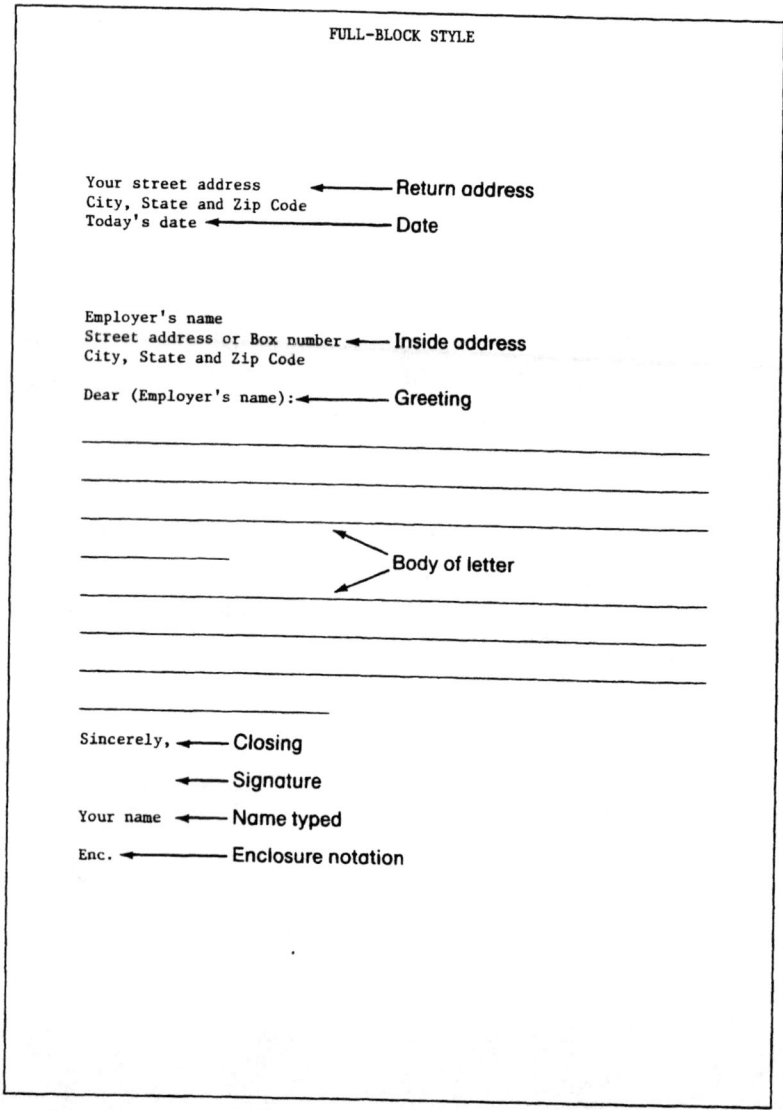

FULL-BLOCK STYLE

```
Your street address      ◄──── Return address
City, State and Zip Code
Today's date ◄──────────────── Date


Employer's name
Street address or Box number ◄── Inside address
City, State and Zip Code

Dear (Employer's name): ◄────── Greeting

─────────────────────────────────
─────────────────────────────────

─────────────────────       ╲
                             ╱ Body of letter
─────────────────────────────────

─────────────────────────────────
─────────────────────────────────


Sincerely, ◄──── Closing

          ◄──── Signature

Your name ◄──── Name typed

Enc. ◄───────── Enclosure notation
```

MODIFIED BLOCK STYLE

Return address ⟶ Your street and address
City, State and Zip Code
Date ⟶ Today's date

Employer's name
Street address or Box number ⟵ Inside address
City, State and Zip Code

Dear (Employer's name) ⟵ Greeting

Body of letter

Closing ⟶ Sincerely,

Signature ⟶

Name typed ⟶ Your name

When to Apply in Writing

Some employers prefer that you contact them by mail when applying for a job. If you look at the help-wanted section in the newspaper you will notice ads such as this:

> HELP WANTED: Sales Clerk,
> APPLY TO: Jean E. Thompson, Assistant Manager, Discount Shoe Outlet, P.O. Box 46, Chicago, Illinois 60606

Because the employer does not list a street address or telephone number, you will have to write a letter of application in order to be considered. Your letter of application should tell the employer three things:

- the position for which you are applying
- your qualifications for the position
- your interest in arranging an interview

The application letter does not have to be long or detailed. Let the resume that accompanies your letter tell the employer about your qualifications and experience.

Sample Letters of Application

Before writing your letter of application, study the samples on the following pages.

21 Newark Avenue
Gary, Indiana 62098
May 24, 1987

Jean E. Thompson
Assistant Manager
Discount Shoe Outlet
P.O. Box 46
Chicago, Illinois 60606

Dear Ms. Thompson:

I would like to apply for the sales clerk position advertised in today's Chicago Tribune. Next week I will graduate from Lew Wallace High School and could begin work immediately.

As you will note from the enclosed resume, during the past two years I have worked as a part-time clerk at the Busy Bee Grocery Store. My duties involved stocking shelves, assisting customers, and preparing orders for delivery.

As a result of my experience with customers, I feel very qualified for your sales clerk position and would like to arrange an interview at your earliest convenience.

Sincerely,

Denise Karamanis

Enc.

Floral Designer
for small shop. Must be available some weekend hours. Driver's license necessary. Apply in writing to: The Flower Pot, 1201 Office Park Rd., Danbury, CT 06812

1261 49th Avenue, Apt. 8B
Danbury, Connecticut 06811
November 2, 1987

The Flower Pot
1201 Office Park Road
Danbury, Connecticut 06812

Dear Sir or Madam:

I am very interested in being considered for the Floral Designer's job available at the The Flower Pot. I am currently seeking a position that would combine my interests in color and design with the opportunity to work with people.

My schedule is flexible and would allow me to work day, evening, or weekend hours as needed. Your ad mentions that a driver's license is necessary. In addition to being a licensed driver, I am very familiar with the city.

My resume is enclosed for your review. I would welcome the opportunity to interview for this position.

Sincerely yours,

James Haverkamp

Enc.

MANAGER TRAINEE
Captain Coco's
Seeking energetic person
w/good personality. Must have
restaurant & some cooking
experience. Send resume to
Bill Coco, 3 Rodeo Drive,
Laramie, WY 82071

---

16 Brandt Towers
Central Community College
Laramie, Wyoming 82071
July 15, 1987

Bill Coco
Captain Coco's
3 Rodeo Drive
Laramie, Wyoming 82071

Dear Mr. Coco:

Please consider me an applicant for the position of Manager
Trainee advertised in the July 14 edition of the Laramie Post.
I enjoy the restaurant business, and I am eager to become
involved in managing the day-to-day operations of the business.

Since high school I have held part-time and summer jobs in
restaurants in the Laramie area. As the enclosed resume
indicates, I started as a dishwasher in a supper club, was
promoted to chef's assistant, and remained in that position
for two summers. While attending Central Community College,
I have been employed part time as a cook in the Student Union
sandwich shop.

At the end of the month I will finish my Associate of Arts
degree in general studies and could begin working immediately.
I would be very interested in discussing the Manager Trainee's
duties and responsibilities with you. I can come in for an
interview at any time convenient for you. I look forward to
hearing from you.

Sincerely,

Philip Horton

Enc.

Addressing Envelopes

Addressing your envelope finishes your writing assignment. Do it just as neatly as you wrote your letter. For all business correspondence, put your full name and address in the upper left corner of the envelope and type the employer's name and address near the center of the envelope. Always include the ZIP Code, even if you have to go to the post office to look it up in the ZIP Code Directory.

```
Denise Karamanis
21 Newark Avenue
Gary, Indiana 62098



                    Jean E. Thompson
                    Assistant Manager
                    Discount Shoe Outlet
                    P.O. Box 46
                    Chicago, Illinois  60606
```

Folding Business Letters

Folding your letter properly is an important step in the application process, too. You have spent time creating an attractive letter. Don't ruin its effect by not taking the time to fold it neatly.

For all business letters it is preferable to use a large (No. 10) envelope rather than the standard (No. 6) one used for most personal letters. The diagrams on the following page show the correct way to fold letters for each of these envelopes: No. 6 (6½″ × 3⅝″) and No. 10 (9½″ × 4⅛″).

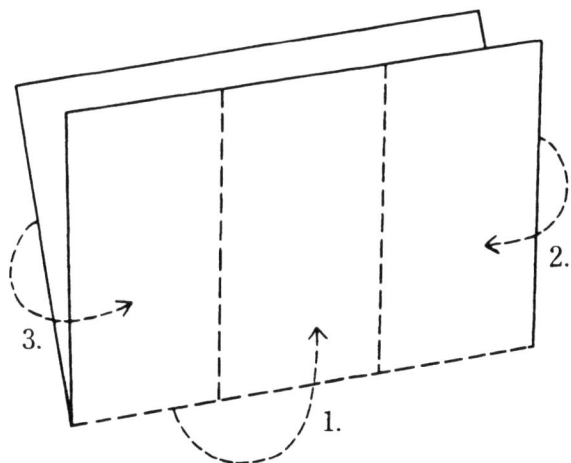

For small envelope (No. 6)
1. Fold bottom to within ½" of top.
2. Fold right third to the left.
3. Fold left third to the right.

For large envelope (No. 10)
1. Fold up bottom third.
2. Fold top third over bottom third.

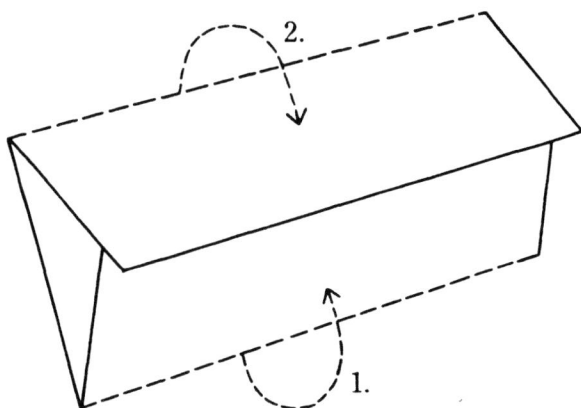

Make Forms and Letters Work for You

Filling out application forms and writing business letters takes time. It's easy to come up with a whole battery of excuses to avoid writing letters:

- I don't know what to say.
- I haven't got time.
- I can't type—or I don't have a typewriter.
- I'd rather just pick up the phone.

If any of these phrases sound familiar to you, you are not alone. But don't let these excuses keep you from pursuing job opportunities.

The information and the samples in this chapter should help you to get started. Good letters don't just happen by accident. You may have to write several drafts of a letter before you feel it is ready to be sent to an employer. However, once you have written one good application letter, you can use it as a model for other ones. Adapting the letter to specific openings will be relatively easy.

Employers use application forms and letters to select the people they want to interview. So it is to your advantage to complete each form accurately and neatly and to write the best letter you can. If you use these papers to make yourself look good to employers, you can come that much closer to getting the job you want.

Steps to Looking Good

Step One: Identifying and understanding your needs, your interests, your skills and attributes, and making a commitment to your job search.

Step Two: Knowing how to prepare a resume and understanding how to use it.

Step Three: *Communicating with employers by providing information on application forms and by writing purposeful letters.*

Chapter Review

Application Forms

Why are application forms important? How does an employer use an application form? What kinds of questions will be included? Why do I need to read it over before I turn it in? Does an application form take the place of my resume?

Letters

What are the characteristics of a business letter? What are the parts of a business letter? When should I apply in writing? What should my letter tell an employer? What does an employer look for? How can my letter help me get an interview?

4 Looking Good at Interviews

Employers hire the people who make the best overall impression. Because the **interview** is the most important part of any job search, you must look good at an interview in order to be successful. Interviewing is not always easy. The tension and stress of being in an unfamiliar situation can sometimes make it difficult to act naturally. Don't try to be someone you're not. Most employers can easily spot someone who is phony or not sincere. Always be yourself, but be sure the interviewer sees you at your best.

Tips for Looking Good

Before you can even say hello you have already told the interviewer many things about yourself. From head to toe, appearance talks. You don't need the latest hairstyle or the most expensive clothes to make a good impression. However, you do need to apear well groomed, neat, and appropriately dressed. It's not difficult to project a good image if you think about the following tips.

Grooming

- Make sure your hair, hands, and nails are clean. (If nail polish is used, choose a neutral color—and never go with chipped nails.)
- Go easy on the makeup, perfume, or after-shave.

- Keep jewelry to a minimum—too much is
distracting.
- Put your sunglasses in your pocket or purse—not
on your face.

Clothing

- Avoid wild patterns or designs.
- Steer clear of low-cut blouses or T-shirts.
- Be cautious of wearing blue jeans. (If you do think
they're appropriate for the job, wear your best
pair.)
- Check your shoes to make certain they are clean or
polished.

Rushing out to buy new clothes for interviews isn't necessary. Take a good look at the things you have hanging in
your closet. Chances are you have everything you need. Use
common sense in selecting your interview outfit. Imagine
how you would expect to be dressed if you were hired. For
example, suppose you are applying for a sales clerk position
in an expensive clothing store. Then it would be a good idea
to wear one of your better outfits. On the other hand, you
would want to pick a more casual outfit if you were going
for an interview at a sporting goods store.

Many businesses expect their employees to wear uniforms at work. This is especially true in fast-food places.
Wearing a sport coat and tie or an expensive dress is not
necessary for such interviews. Pants or a skirt and a nice
shirt or blouse are entirely appropriate.

Whatever you wear, it should be clean and neatly
pressed, and something you feel comfortable wearing. Your
grooming habits and your choice of clothing can make a
difference in your job search. It is always safer to be conser-
vative in appearance than to adopt the latest fad or fashion
trend.

Don't Go Empty-handed

A good way to impress an employer is to come prepared for an interview. You should be ready to tell the employer what you have done and perhaps show examples of your skills.

Not all job seekers will take along the same things. But the following materials are some good suggestions:

- photographs or drawings of completed projects from your previous employment or from classes such as home economics, industrial arts, or mechanical drawing

- samples of units completed in bookkeeping or other office-related courses

- computer printout of a program you've used or written

- newspaper clippings or other written materials that have some connection to you or your workplace

It's helpful to have materials at hand in case the interviewer does express an interest in what you have done. Be ready to use them as illustrations if the opportunity presents itself. But don't expect that to happen at every interview. And don't try to force it if the interviewer doesn't ask for them. Not all employers will have the time or the interest to look at samples of your work. Be ready for those who do—but don't plan a presentation around them.

Whether or not you take any work samples with you, you should always make sure that you have the following items:

- a copy of your resume to leave with the interviewer

- your Social Security card and other identification

- pencil, pen, and paper

- some money for emergencies (at least
  telephone change)

Don't just cram these items into your purse or pocket. Put them in a folder, notebook, or other convenient package so they will be easily available but not noticeable.

When Scott Crawford applied for his job as assistant to a cabinetmaker, he knew that he couldn't take his actual projects with him to the interview. Instead, he took photographs of the bookcase he built in shop class. He also took pictures of some other items he had made as gifts for his mother. Knowing that he could show examples of his work made Scott more confident at his interview. And it made it easier for him to remember the things he wanted to tell the cabinetmaker about his skills. Preparing these materials beforehand made Scott appear organized and serious about wanting the job.

Do a Little Homework

Knowing as much as you can about a company before you go to an interview will make you look good to an employer. Gathering information in advance will help you to:

- be ready for the interviewer's questions
- think about questions you want to ask
- look and feel confident

Finding out basic facts about an employer can be accomplished by talking to people or reading about a company. If you know someone who works (or has worked) for that employer, there are several things you can find out. You can learn what the various people in the company do, what the hours are, how the work shifts are organized, how the employees are supervised, and what kind of clothing they wear. You can also ask about the amount of money you could expect to earn, opportunities for advancement, training programs, and company benefits.

If you don't know anyone who has direct knowledge of the employer, your homework may be a little more difficult. Personnel offices of large companies sometimes have pamphlets or other printed information available about the company. Your public library may have information about some companies. Counselors and placement advisers in your school can also be sources of information about possible employers. Finally, you can check with your local chamber of commerce for some basic facts about certain employers.

The effort you make to **research** a possible employer will take a little time. But it is time well spent. Even having a small amount of information is better than not knowing anything about a possible employer.

Interview Dos and Don'ts

In addition to being organized, there are many other ways to look good during an interview. The attitude and behavior you demonstrate can be just as important. Use the tips in the following list of "Dos and Don'ts" to help you make a good impression.

Dos

Be Prepared Having a successful interview means being prepared. Be prepared not only to answer questions but to ask them as well. Most interviewers will ask you if you have any questions—about the job, the company, or anything else that has come up during the interview. Be prepared to ask a few intelligent questions. It shows you have a serious interest in the company—and the job.

Be on Time   There is no excuse for being late for an interview. However, being too early is not a good idea, either. Having to wait in the employer's office may not be convenient and can make you more nervous than you already are. Arriving about five minutes early gives you time to find the office, catch your breath, and collect your thoughts.

Be Independent   Go alone. Bringing someone with you to an interview can give the impression that you are too dependent on others. Employers want to hire people who can function on their own. If friends or relatives drive you to the interview, ask them to come back after the interview is finished.

Be Courteous   The first person you meet may not be the interviewer. If you are greeted by a receptionist, state clearly who you are and why you are there. For example, "I'm Mary Smith and I have an interview appointment with Mr. Jones at two o'clock." Or, "I'm Mary Smith and I was asked to come for an interview at two o'clock." Always be polite to receptionists. While they do not make the hiring decisions, interviewers may ask for their impressions. When you do meet the interviewer, remember to smile, shake hands if the interviewer offers to, and wait for an invitation to be seated.

Be Alert   Pay attention. Listen carefully so that you hear what the interviewer is telling you about the job. Eye contact is very important. Of course you don't want to stare at the interviewer. But not meeting the person's eyes will make the interviewer feel very uncomfortable about you.

Be Serious   Interviews take time—everyone's time. Make the best use of your interview by showing the employer that you are interested in the job. Don't act silly, bored, or impatient. You need to come across as a sincere, responsible, reliable person.

Don'ts

Rush   When you are asked a question, take the time to think about your response. Rushing your answer can lead to incomplete or incorrect answers. Don't keep checking your watch. It gives the impression that you have better things to do. Relax and let the interviewer control the situation.

Create Distractions   Keep all distractions to a minimum. You will want to concentrate on what the interviewer is telling and asking you. Don't smoke, chew gum, suck on breath mints—or do anything such as tapping your foot or fidgeting in a chair. Interviewers want your full attention. It's easier to concentrate on the interview if you're not distracted by anything.

Get Personal   Never use the interviewer's first name unless you are told to do so. Keep your comments businesslike. Never make the mistake of flirting. It's not appropriate and will almost guarantee that you will not be hired.

Speak Negatively   Nobody wants to hire a complainer. Negative reactions can give the impression that you are hard to satisfy. Don't say bad things about former **supervisors** or employers, and don't even complain about the bad weather or the rush-hour traffic. When answering a question or making a statement always try to be positive.

Say Too Much   Stick to the subject. Don't waste time talking about topics that are not related to the job. Monopolizing the conversation, telling jokes, or boasting tells the employer that you are more interested in yourself than you are in the job.

Worry Too Much If you appear calm, you're halfway there. Nervousness is natural in an interview, and there may not be anything you can do about it. But you can cover your feelings by looking composed.

Unexpected Interviews

> *Barbara Rogers found her first job in a candy shop by going from store to store asking about job possibilities. Barbara had not contacted any employers in advance. So she realized that many of the people she talked with would simply say that no jobs were available. But Barbara felt that there was always the chance her timing might be right and she might get an on-the-spot interview.*
>
> *In order to make a good impression Barbara wore a skirt and blouse that she felt would be appropriate for any of the stores in the area. She also carried copies of her resume. And she was sure to include her Social Security card in her billfold before she left home. She wasn't hired at the first shop she visited—or even the sixth. But the tenth store she went into needed someone immediately. They hired her for part-time work, evenings and Saturdays.*

Anyone can walk into a store, restaurant, or office, just as Barbara did, and ask if there are any job openings. But not everyone does a good job of communicating with an employer. Unscheduled interviews are usually brief. In order to use these few minutes to your advantage, you must be prepared to make a good first impression. This means giving the important information about yourself, answering the employer's questions, and asking appropriate questions of your own.

At the Interview

What Will You Talk About?

It's only natural to be nervous and excited about an interview—especially if it's your first one. You're wondering what the interviewer will ask you and what you should say. Your interview will be easier, and you'll be able to make a better impression, if you know what to expect.

Most interviewers realize that you are nervous. So, many of them will start by making small talk about the weather, sports, or some other unrelated topic. Others may begin by telling you about the job. However the interview begins, you can expect to be asked a number of questions. Be ready for them. You can't anticipate every question you might be asked. But you can be sure that you will need answers to some of the following basic questions:

- Why do you want to work here?
- Tell me about your last job.
- Have you ever had experience with this type of work?
- Why do you think you would be successful in this job?
- What are your strengths? Weaknesses?
- How would you **evaluate** your performance on past jobs?
- What did you like best about your previous boss? Least?
- What are your goals? Short range? Long range?
- What class did you enjoy most in school? Least? Why?
- What activities have you participated in?
- What do you like to do in your spare time?

- Tell me about yourself.
- How would you describe yourself to another person?
- Tell me about someone you respect.
- Tell me something you are proud of.
- Are you interested in part-time or full-time employment?
- If this job requires traveling, do you have your own transportation?
- Would you rather work with others or by yourself? Why?
- How would you define a good worker?

It's a good idea to think about possible answers to these questions before you go to a job interview. Don't try to memorize your answers. But do think about what you want to tell the interviewer—and remember to use positive expressions. Being prepared before the interview will help you feel confident and look good to an employer.

Questions You Should Not Be Asked

You should also be aware that there are some questions you should not be asked during an interview. Federal and state guidelines forbid questions about race, religion, or national origin. Other questions which do not relate to your qualifications for the job are not appropriate and, in some cases, are in violation of state and federal guidelines. Some examples of these questions are:

- Where were you born?
- What is your father's occupation?
- What church do you attend?
- What is your native language?
- Do you live in an apartment or a house?
- Do you live alone?

- Are you married?
- Do you have any children?
- Do you use alcohol or drugs?
- Have you ever been arrested?

Your responses to these kinds of questions may vary depending upon the situation. For example, you may believe that the employer is merely trying to make you feel at ease by asking about your family. If so, you may respond differently than if you suspect that the questions may be part of a policy of **discrimination.**

You do have choices in dealing with personal questions not related to your qualifications for the job. You can simply give the information as requested. Or you can state that the question is not related to the job and refuse to answer it. Or you can ask the interviewer why the information is being requested and then decide whether you wish to answer. If you decide not to answer a question, be polite but firm.

In preparing for interviews, you should consider the possibility that you might be faced with questions that are not appropriate. Thinking about these questions ahead of time will give you the confidence to respond clearly and without embarrassment.

What Questions Should You Ask?

Because an interview is an exchange of information, you should also have in mind some questions you want answered. Some interviewers will tell you everything you need to know. Others might not get around to some of the details. If something has been left out, feel free to ask about it. During the interview, keep a mental checklist of what has been said. Some of the basic questions you might need or want to ask are:

- When does the job start?
- What will my work schedule be?

- How far in advance will I be scheduled?
- Who will supervise my work?
- Will my duties vary?
- Will special clothing or uniforms be required?
- How many people work here?
- Is there a possibility for promotion?
- Would I be replacing someone, or is this a new job?

Asking About Pay

Of course you will want to know what the hourly wage or monthly salary will be. Most interviewers will provide this information sometime during the interview. But if it is overlooked, don't be afraid to ask what your pay will be. Just don't let that be the first or the only question you ask. The interviewer might then get the impression that you are interested only in the money and not in the job.

Don't Talk Yourself Out of a Job

Knowing how to end an interview is almost as important as knowing how to begin one. Don't make the mistake of prolonging the conversation once the interviewer has begun to draw things to a close. Most interviewers will give you signals that the interview is over. The interviewer may set your application aside, push his or her chair away from the desk, or even stand up. Once you see one or more of these signs, you must wrap up what you are saying and prepare to leave. If you do have one final question that you feel is important, take the time to ask it. Before you leave there are two things you should always find out:

- when the hiring decision will be made
- when you will be notified

Leave on a Positive Note

Don't rush out of the room. An interview is never complete until you express your appreciation for the time the interviewer has spent with you. It's also a good opportunity to tell the interviewer once again that you are interested in the job. Be sure you know the interviewer's name and, if necessary, ask how it is spelled. You'll need this information later on. Remember to smile and try to leave with the positive impression that you made at the beginning.

Looking Back

Record the Facts

After the interview, take a little time to make a few notes about what you learned. Jot down such things as the duties of the position, when the job starts, what the hours will be, the starting salary, and if there is any opportunity for advancement. In addition, always record the time of the interview, where it was held, and the name of the interviewer. All of this information will be very helpful if you are interviewing for several jobs. It's easy to get confused after a number of different interviews. But if you keep simple records it will take just a minute to refresh your memory.

> *Tony Dellos has scheduled several interviews in the next three weeks. He's already a little nervous about the whole idea of interviewing. He knows it's easy to forget important details when you're thinking about a number of different things. So, Tony has come up with a simple method to keep track of the basic facts about each interview. All*

*the information he needs can be quickly recorded
on this file card he has prepared.*

Employer _____

Address _____

Interviewer _____ Phone _____

Date/time of interview _____

Job title/duties:

Starting date:

Hours/schedule:

Wages/salary:

Comments:

This card shows the information Tony jotted down after
his first interview:

Employer _Capitol Cameras_

Address _1146 Sycamore St._

Interviewer _Tom Nagel_   Phone _533-6109_

Date/time of interview _August 6, 2p.m._

Job title/duties: _Sales clerk- cameras, film, etc. – take orders
                   for developing prints_
Starting date: _Soon as possible_

Hours/schedule: _10-6 – Some Sat's. & Sun's._

Wages/salary: _$ 4⁵⁰/hr._

Comments: _Should decide by Saturday. Busy place !_

While you are recording the facts about the interview, you
should also take a few minutes to think about the kinds of
questions you were asked and how you answered them. If

you think you gave an especially good answer to a question, make a note of it. Chances are you'll be asked a similar question in another interview. You might also write down any questions you found hard to handle. Then you can give some thought to how you might make a better response to similar questions in future interviews.

Review Your Impressions

Everyone feels relieved after an interview. And you might also feel something of a letdown after the nervousness has passed. It's natural to be dissatisfied with your performance. When the interview is over, it's easy to think of things you might have done differently. Don't be too hard on yourself. Don't worry too much about the impression you made. Instead, consider what went well and then move on to things you might improve on. For example:

- Was I late?
- Did I talk too much? Too little?
- Did I find it hard to establish eye contact?
- Did I speak too softly?
- Did I get confused?
- Did I know when to leave?

These are things you can do something about. And it's better for you to evaluate your performance than to think about your chances of getting the job. You simply do not have enough information about the qualifications of the other applicants to know whether you will be hired.

Follow-up Letters

After the interview is over, there is one more important thing for you to do. It won't take more than a few minutes.

And it could greatly increase your chances of getting the job. Writing a letter thanking the employer for the interview and expressing your interest in the job gives you one more chance to look good.

Be sure to take the time to write this letter. Many other applicants will not. Seeing your name one more time will help the interviewer remember you. It will also tell the employer that you are serious about the position. And it will show that you are thoughtful and willing to take the time to follow through. Try to write your letter immediately after the interview. If you wait too long, your letter will have little effect on the interviewer's hiring decision.

Follow-up letters should be brief. Always use a standard business letter style and standard 8½" × 11" paper. Address your letter to the person who conducted the interview, and be sure the person's name is spelled correctly. Proofread your letter carefully to catch any spelling errors.

Sample Follow-up Letters

The following sample letters show how easy it is to write an interview follow-up letter. Note that no matter what type of position you've applied for, all follow-up letters should include a final thank-you for the opportunity to interview for the job; another expression of your interest in the job; and a request that you be informed when a hiring decision is made.

Rt. 3, Box 52
North Branch, Minnesota 55056
March 2, 1987

Donald Wheeler
Texaco Service
North Branch, Minnesota 55056

Dear Mr. Wheeler:

Thank you for giving me the opportunity this morning to
discuss with you the senior mechanic's position you have
available. I am quite interested in the job, and I feel
that my previous experience qualifies me for consideration.

I look forward to hearing from you regarding your decision
sometime next week.

Sincerely,

Craig Crawford

4732 Nord Drive
Cedar Rapids, Iowa 52405
June 16, 1987

Nancy Piper
Area Supervisor
Midwest Life Insurance Company
23 First Avenue N.W.
Cedar Rapids, Iowa 52406

Dear Ms. Piper:

Thank you for the time and consideration shown to
me during my interview for the clerk-typist job
on Friday, June 14. I feel confident I could
handle the responsibilities of the position
and would like you to consider me as a serious
applicant.

I look forward to hearing from you in the near
future.

Sincerely,

Michelle Lewin

320 Fourth Avenue
Arcata, California 95521
May 2, 1987

Mary Ann Nabors
District Manager
Western Athletic Supplies
762 Billie Street
Eureka, California 95501

Dear Ms. Nabors:

As a result of our meeting on Thursday, April 30, I am
even more enthusiastic about the possibility of working as
a sales representative for Western Athletic Supplies. I was
particularly impressed with your description of the training
program for new representatives. I am sure that with my
previous retail sales experience I would utilize this
training very effectively.

As you know from our conversation, athletics has been an
important part of my life. Because of my familiarity with
many of Western's products, I would welcome the opportunity
to promote Western Athletic Supplies to buyers in northern
California.

I enjoyed meeting you and appreciated the opportunity
to interview for this position. I anticipate hearing from
you regarding your hiring decision within the next few days.

Sincerely,

Mildred Kemp

The Countdown

You can expect to wait a few days, in some cases even weeks, before you know if you have been selected for the job. If you haven't heard from the employer in a reasonable amount of time, it is appropriate to check to see if a decision has been made.

> *Two weeks ago, Karin Meade was interviewed for a job with an accounting firm. She was told that other people would be interviewed, but that she would hear about the job within ten days. Fourteen days have now passed. Although Karin has continued her job search, she would like to know whether she is still being considered.*
>
> *Before calling to inquire, Karin has checked the note card she completed after the interview for the name of the interviewer, the exact title of the job, and the date of the interview. It has taken Karin two days to work up the nerve to make the telephone call. She knows that she will be disappointed if she learns the position has been filled by someone else. But she'd rather know where she stands than to wait and worry.*

Not every interview will result in a job offer. If you learn that you were not chosen, don't be too discouraged. You can always let the employer know that you would like to be considered for future openings.

The Job Offer

When you are selected for a job, most employers will call to give you the news. Being offered a job is always satisfying and may be very exciting. But it can also mean that you have some decisions to make. If you have interviewed for only one job, your decision may be an easy one. If you have had several interviews, however, your decision may be more difficult. This is especially true if the offer you receive does not come from the job that looked most interesting.

Some employers will want to know immediately if you are going to accept their job offer. Others will give you a day or two to consider it. If you need time to think about it, ask the employer how much time you have to make your decision. For part-time or temporary jobs, you should usually be prepared to accept or to turn down an offer when it is made.

If the employer is able to give you some time to make your decision, you can check to see if you are still being considered for the job you really want. A phone call to the preferred employer will usually help you to decide. You might learn that applications are still being accepted, or that a hiring decision will not be made for several days. If that is the case, you'll have a tough decision to make. Are you willing to turn down the offer you have received on the chance that you will receive a better one?

Be cautious. Never put off an answer to a job offer unless it's for a very good reason. And never request time to consider an offer without expressing your appreciation for the offer.

Steps to Looking Good

Step One: Identifying and understanding your needs, your interests, your skills and attributes, and making a commitment to your job search.

Step Two: Knowing how to prepare a resume and understanding how to use it.

Step Three: Communicating with employers by providing information on application forms and by writing purposeful letters.

Step Four: *Taking the time to prepare for interviews, knowing how to conduct yourself at interviews, and following through after interviews.*

Chapter Review

Appearance

Why is appearance so important? Do employers judge you on how you look? Are there things to avoid? Is there one right way to look for every job interview? Will I have to buy a new outfit for each interview?

Being Prepared

How can I demonstrate my skills? Will employers want to see samples of my work? What are the important items I should take to every interview? What should I know about the company? How can I find the information I need?

Dos and Don'ts

Should I take anyone with me to an interview? How do I introduce myself to the receptionist? How important is eye contact? What kind of impression should I leave with the employer? Should I try to make friends with the interviewer? How much should I say during the interview? What do I do if I'm nervous?

Interview Questions

Am I prepared for the basic questions? What can I expect to be asked? How can I respond to questions that are not appropriate? What questions should I ask?

Follow-Through

How can I remember what happened? How should I review my interview performance? What is the purpose of a follow-up letter? When should I check back with an employer?

Job Offers

How will I learn if I've been selected? Should I accept the first job offer? Can I have time to consider the job?

5 Overcoming Obstacles

All job seekers need to know how to look good on paper and in person. Designing attractive resumes, writing effective letters, and making good impressions at interviews are important parts of every job search. But sometimes learning to do these things is not enough. Many people must also overcome **obstacles** of one kind or another which can affect their chances for finding a job.

If you've dropped out of school or been fired from a previous job, this can sometimes cause problems in a job search. Coping with a physical or mental **handicap** or having a criminal record are two other circumstances that will affect your job search. Millions of people are faced with one or more of these obstacles. If you are one of them, you will have to deal with your situation directly. Ignoring these problems will not make them go away. Nor can you pretend they won't influence possible employers. But these obstacles need not keep you from being considered for jobs.

Your attitude is *very* important. If you see your particular situation as hopeless, it probably will be. No employer will be able to see beyond the obstacle unless you do. No interviewer will see you as a productive worker unless you are convinced that you can be.

Even with one or more obstacles, you can still make yourself look good to employers. Start by being honest with yourself. That will allow you to be honest with employers and to see your problems in the proper light. Keep in mind

79

that you are not alone. Millions of others have faced
obstacles like yours and have managed to succeed in spite
of them.

If You're a Dropout

There are many reasons people leave school without a
diploma. Some people are bored, and some have academic or
personal problems. Others quit because of **peer pressure.**
And still others leave because they need to support themselves or other family members. Some dropouts never plan
to finish high school. Others see dropping out as a temporary
situation and fully intend to return to school. And many
people find they would rather attend an alternative school
or obtain a high school equivalency diploma by taking
classes at a later time. (The tests for General Educational
Development [GED] are given several times a year in most
areas.) Whatever your situation, you must be prepared to
deal with this issue on application forms and in interviews.

All application forms ask for information about your
education. Always complete this section fully, giving names
of schools and dates of attendance. Put a dash (—) in the
column for the year the diploma was awarded to show that
you have not completed high school. Do not leave this
section blank. You need to let the employer know you've
not left answers off your application on purpose.

Many employers will ask you questions about your
education and your reasons for leaving school. These are
proper questions. You must be prepared to answer them
without hesitating and without being negative. Speaking
negatively about school subjects or teachers will never be to
your advantage. Concentrate instead on your abilities and
your eagerness to be a good worker.

Maria Brown dropped out of high school in her junior year. She is now looking for a full-time job. At her first interview she had difficulty with questions about why she decided to leave school. Without thinking, she told the interviewer that the classes were boring and she felt she was wasting her time. The interviewer then asked if Maria thought she would find work as uninteresting as school. Maria realized that by expressing a lack of interest in school, she had given the interviewer the impression that she might not be an enthusiastic worker.

Maria's feelings about school have not changed. But she is going to choose her words more carefully at future interviews. Instead of using the word "boring," she is going to explain that—at least for the time being—she would find working more relevant and meaningful.

Explain the Reason

You may have dropped out of school because you were bored or because your friends had also dropped out. If so, you need to tell the employer that the time you were putting into school was not productive and perhaps you wanted to earn some money. Employers will hesitate to hire you if they feel you will not take an interest in your work.

Suppose that you dropped out because of difficulty with your studies or because of some personal problem. It is not necessary to give possible employers every detail of your decision. You can simply explain that earning some money had become more important than continuing in school. If you dropped out to help support your family or to pay your own living expenses, you can let the employer know that your decision to drop out was purely economic.

If you intend to return to school to complete your education, you should be sure that the employer understands your goals.

The kinds of employment available to you as a dropout may be more limited than if you had earned your high school diploma. However, you can certainly apply for any of the kinds of jobs usually held by people your age. Jobs that do not require a high school diploma can give you the opportunity to establish a solid work record. You can then use your employment experience to find better jobs in the future.

If You've Been Fired

Getting fired from a job doesn't mean you'll never be able to find another one. It does mean that you need to understand the situation—including the reason you were fired. And you need to think about how you will discuss the loss of your job with future employers.

People are fired for many different reasons. It's not impossible to be let go after only a day or two of work. The employer may realize that a mistake has been made and you simply are not suited for the job. It is also possible to be fired after months or even years of employment. Some reasons people are fired include:

- lack of enthusiasm
- being consistently late for work
- constantly complaining
- rudeness
- dishonesty
- refusing to obey supervisors
- poor attitude
- poor job performance

If you were fired, you probably know the reason. Most employers give warnings or specific directions for performance improvement. If the situation is not corrected, the employer may have no choice but to fire the worker.

> *Eight months ago, Kim Long was hired as a clerk in the business office of a large hospital. On several occasions, Kim arrived late to work. Each time she had an excuse, such as, "My alarm didn't go off," "I had car trouble," or "I got caught in traffic." Because she worked in a large office, Kim felt that her work station would be covered by other clerks and her being late would not be a problem. Kim was a good worker and had received positive performance evaluations. However, after she received two warnings about being late and made no clear effort to correct the situation, Kim was fired.*

If you are fired and do not know the reason, ask your supervisor to give you a reason. It's not an easy question to ask. And sometimes it's not an easy question for an employer to answer. But you will need this information in order to deal with future employment possibilities.

Employers are going to want to know about your past work record. They may ask for this information on an application form or during the interview. The application form might ask your reasons for leaving a previous job. Instead of going into detail, or using the word "fired," you can simply write "let go" as the reason for leaving. It doesn't sound as negative or severe and may give you a chance to explain the situation in an interview.

Be Positive

You can be sure that any future employer will ask questions about your previous work experience. So, you will need to give some thought to how you will respond to questions about a job from which you were fired. If you want to get hired for a new job it is important that you avoid complaining about your previous work or employer. Don't blame others for your situation or make excuses for your past performance. Find a way to talk about your previous experience that will show you have the ability to succeed on a new job.

Some of the following phrases could be helpful as you think about your situation.

- I was not ready for the responsibility of my first job.
- I didn't realize how important it was to be on time.
- I found it hard to balance my work and other activities.
- I was not aware of my supervisor's authority.
- My family situation at the time created transportation problems.
- The problems were caused by personality conflicts.

You may need to develop even more complete responses to questions regarding your previous employment. Never lie or distort the facts. Try to build on the positive parts of your former job. And stress to a possible employer that you have the skills, interest, and desire to succeed in a new position.

If You're Handicapped

Whatever your handicap, it's not necessarily an obstacle to finding a job. But it will influence the way you approach your job search. Today, there are more handicapped people in the work force than ever before. Handicaps vary in degree and in visibility. Some are obvious, and others are hidden. They include:

- visual **impairment**
- hearing impairment
- epilepsy
- cerebral palsy
- multiple sclerosis
- diabetes
- kidney disease
- physical impairment
- brain damage
- learning disabilities
- chemical dependency

Whatever the nature of your handicap, you must be prepared to discuss it with possible employers. Employers have a right to know about any physical or mental condition that would affect your job performance. Application forms often request information about handicaps. Your response to this kind of question should be clear and brief. In order that employers can understand the nature of your disability, avoid using complicated medical terms. State any limitations in terms an employer will understand.

You should know that some employers require tests which can reveal chemical dependencies. Some companies conduct preemployment tests. And some employers require periodic testing for some or all employees.

Introducing the Topic

One of the most difficult decisions for a handicapped job seeker is when or how to inform a possible employer of the handicap. There is no single answer. Some people prefer to inform the employer in advance of an interview. This can be done either by mentioning the handicap in a telephone call or in a letter of application. Others prefer to wait until they have the opportunity to meet the employer in person.

> *John Greenwald knows that first impressions are important. The fact that he is confined to a wheelchair makes an obvious statement. In order to lessen the interviewer's apprehension, John introduces himself, then grins and says, "You won't need to find me a chair—I brought my own." John's lighthearted comment introduces the topic of his handicap and shows his willingness to discuss his condition as it relates to the job.*

Many employers are uncomfortable in dealing with handicapped people. Some are unsure of what questions to ask or even how to introduce the topic. If necessary, be ready to talk about your condition and to explain how your skills can be a benefit to the employer. Don't dwell on your disability. You want to emphasize your qualifications for the job and your ability to handle it. But you may need to control the discussion, so that the employer's stated or unspoken questions about your ability to function in the job are answered. The following are some questions you can expect to be asked:

- Would special accommodations or equipment in your work station be required?
- How have others reacted to your handicap—in school or on other jobs?
- Will you need any special assistance for routine parts of the job?

Sometimes these questions will not be asked directly by employers. However, you should take the responsibility to tell the interviewer what you can do and what you will need in order to perform the duties of the job. Getting hired depends on whether you can convince the employer that you have the necessary skills to do the job. One way to do that is to use examples from your school background or experience on other jobs to show how you were able to handle your responsibilities.

If You Have a Criminal Record

Individuals with criminal records often have serious employment problems. It is no secret that some employers simply will not consider applicants who have been convicted of a crime. There *are* employers, however, who will give all applicants the opportunity to interview for positions. One of the most important parts of your job search is your ability to present your situation accurately and to demonstrate a positive attitude.

> *Dwight Watson was convicted of auto theft when he was nineteen. Because he had no previous criminal record, he was sentenced to a year in a halfway house and a year's **probation**. Dwight is prepared to tell possible employers what his offense was and what his responsibilities were at the halfway house. He also wants to stress the good work he did at his last job—part-time employment in the kitchen of a local restaurant. Dwight knows that in order to present a positive image, he has to get over his past problems. He has to concentrate on his work record, his desire to succeed, and his determination to obtain a full-time job.*

A criminal record is not something you can hide from possible employers. Application forms often request information about criminal records. The question may be worded in a number of different ways. It usually asks if you have ever been convicted of a crime and allows space for explanation if the answer is yes. If the question does appear on an application form, you must answer it honestly. Many employers run checks on applicants they are considering to see if they have a criminal record. Some companies even require fingerprinting of all employees.

When you reveal this information to possible employers, you can expect questions about the nature of the offense and whether you are on probation or **parole.** It is wise to have given some thought beforehand to how you are going to respond to these questions. When you state on an application that you have been convicted of an offense, attach a note asking if you may explain your situation in person. This request may allow you to meet the employer. This gives you the chance to answer the employer's questions and to call attention to the skills you have that relate to the job. Questions you could expect include:

- What were you convicted of? When?
- Are you now on probation? Parole?
- Were you in jail?
- May I contact your parole officer?
- What will your parole officer tell me about you?
- Why should I trust you?
- Was this your first offense?
- Are there any terms of your probation that I should be aware of?
- How do you think you will cope with other workers in your department?
- How do you think other workers will react to you?

Some employers will be very blunt about asking questions. Don't be concerned when that happens. Just remember to be honest about your situation at all times. Being completely honest is the first step in showing an employer you have the desire to be a productive and trustworthy employee. It's easy for employers to reject your application unless you can convince them that you are—in spite of what has happened in the past—the best person for the job.

Looking Beyond the Obstacles

Finding a job can sometimes be difficult. And any one of these obstacles can make your job search even more complicated. You must be aware that you may face more job rejections than some other job seekers. Being turned down creates disappointment and frustration, and you may begin to wonder if you'll ever find a job.

No employer will be able to see beyond the obstacle unless you do. Knowing how to deal with your particular obstacle is the key to getting employers to look at your skills and abilities rather than at the problem. Employers want to hire the most qualified person. If you can convince the employer that you are the best person for the job, you can be hired. No apologies or excuses are necessary. Concentrate on your abilities and your strengths, minimize your weaknesses, and deal honestly with yourself and with employers.

You can succeed. It may take longer, and you may have to put more effort into your job search. But you can make it. Don't give up. The only sure way *not* to get a job is to stop looking for one.

If there are obstacles to overcome, finding a job can be even more important. It is an opportunity to prove to yourself and to an employer that you have the skills and determination to succeed. Building a successful work record can help to minimize the problems you've had. And a good work record increases your chances for getting a better job next time.

Steps to Looking Good

Step One: Identifying and understanding your needs, your interests, your skills and attributes, and making a commitment to your job search.

Step Two: Knowing how to prepare a resume and understanding how to use it.

Step Three: Communicating with employers by providing information on application forms and by writing purposeful letters.

Step Four: Taking the time to prepare for interviews, knowing how to conduct yourself at interviews, and following through after interviews.

Step Five: *Overcoming obstacles to finding a job by seeing beyond the problem, dealing with the problem honestly, and maintaining a positive attitude.*

Chapter Review

Dropout

How do I explain to an employer my reasons for leaving school? How do I complete the education section of an application form? How can speaking negatively about school hurt my chances of getting hired?

Fired

Do I know why I lost my job? Why do employers want to know about my previous employment? What am I going to tell the interviewer about my being fired? What must I avoid doing when I talk about my previous job?

Handicap

When do I tell a possible employer about my handicap? How do I introduce the topic? What do I do if an employer seems uncomfortable asking about my handicap? What questions will most employers want answered?

Criminal Record

How do I handle the question, "Have you ever been convicted of a crime?" What should I be prepared to tell an employer about my past? What things must I emphasize during an interview?

6 Where to Look for Jobs

Once you know the steps involved in finding a job, it's time to think about actual job possibilities. Identifying employers may be a fairly simple task. Or it may require that you set aside plenty of time to uncover job leads. Sometimes it depends on the size of your community. In order to increase your chances for success, try to find as many opportunities as you can. Later on, you can focus on the kind of jobs that interest you the most. Remember, the more jobs you are willing to consider, the better your chances of getting hired.

Don't rely on just one method of looking for jobs. Use a variety of sources for gathering job information. You should consider the following:

- classified ads in newspapers
- help wanted signs in shop windows
- public employment agencies
- private employment agencies
- private counselors
- temporary job agencies
- school or college counseling/placement offices
- personnel departments
- personal contacts

The kind of job you are seeking and the amount of time you can devote to your job search are important. These factors will determine the **resources** and contacts you use to discover employment opportunities. The following section describes various resources and methods of finding out about jobs. It also shows how each resource can be used.

Printed Resources

Classified Ads in Newspapers

Almost all newspapers carry a classified ads section. Thousands of jobs are advertised each year by this method alone. The "want ads" are a source that every job seeker needs to know about. Job ads should be checked often.

If your local newspaper has a large circulation, the help wanted ads are likely to be divided into several categories. Some common ones are Professional, Technical, Clerical, Sales, Medical, General, and Domestic. Sunday newspapers are especially good sources of job leads. If an employer intends to advertise a position only once, it will probably appear in the Sunday edition.

Joey Benavides has been watching the daily and Sunday newspaper ads for job leads. One ad that caught his attention was:

Public Service Assistant

WMT-TV

901 Second St. N.E.

Maintain computer files for videotapes, films, slides. Write pub. serv. announcements; order & mount 35mm slides; assist dir. w/book copy; assemble daily logbooks. Type 40 wpm; computer exp. pref. HS dip. req. $4.50/hr. Avail. immed. Apply in person.

The job title sounded interesting, so Joey read the ad carefully to determine if he had the necessary qualifications. Because the ad said to apply in person, Joey knew it was important to get there quickly and to be ready for an on-the-spot interview. He remembered to take along copies of his resume to leave with the employer.

Most newspaper ads will not give very many details about a job. Because of the cost of ads, employers often provide only basic information, such as

- job title or description of duties
- contact person or address
- qualifications or special training required

Also, in order to reduce the length and cost of the ad, many common words or terms are abbreviated. Here are some of the most often used words and their abbreviations.

account	acct.
accounting	acctg.
administrative, administrator	admin.
apartment manager	apt. mgr.
appointment	appt.
as soon as possible	ASAP
assist, assistant	asst.
available	avail.
background	bkgd.
bookkeeper	bkpr.
building	bldg.
calculator	calc.
cathode ray tube	CRT

certificate	cert.
clerk	clk.
college graduate	coll. grad.
computer	comp.
construction	const.
coordinate, coordinator	coord.
department	dept.
diploma	dip.
driver's license	dr. lic.
education	educ.
equipment	equip.
evening	eve.
excellent	exc.
executive	exec.
experience	exp.
full-time	f.t., FT
good	gd.
graduate	grad.
high school graduate	hs. grad, HS grad.
hour	hr.
hourly	hrly.
housekeeper	hskpr.
license, licensed	lic.
manager	mgr.
maximum	max.
minimum	min.
Monday through Friday	M–F
month	mo.
necessary	nec.

need	nd.
operate, operator	oper.
part-time	p.t., PT
permanent	perm.
phone	ph.
possible	poss.
prefer, preferred	pref.
professional	prof.
reference	ref.
representative	rep.
require, required	req.
responsible	resp.
salary	sal.
secretary	sec'y.
supervise	supv.
supervisor	supvr.
technical, technician	tech.
telephone	tel.
telephone switchboard	PBX
temporary	temp.
ten-key adding machine	10-key
thousand	K (as $10,000 = $10K)
train	trn.
type, typing	typ.
week, work	wk.
weekly	wkly.
with	w/
words per minute	w.p.m., wpm
year	yr.

Help Wanted Signs

When you're looking for a job, keep an eye out for help wanted signs in the windows of restaurants, shops, and small businesses. Many employers advertise only in this manner because it's easy, doesn't cost anything, and is effective.

To most people, window signs appear to be a casual way to advertise—but don't be misled. Go in prepared just as you would for an interview that was arranged in advance. You should be appropriately dressed, ready to answer questions or to fill out application forms, and have a resume to leave with the employer.

Employment Agencies

Public Agencies

Each state operates public employment agencies in various towns and cities. Employers of all types and sizes list positions with these state employment services. Part-time, temporary, and summer work opportunities as well as full-time jobs are listed throughout the year. Jobs range from professional positions requiring college degrees and much experience to openings for beginning, inexperienced workers.

Application procedures will vary according to the employer, kind of job, and the required qualifications. Some employment offices can provide you with information and application forms for civil service jobs with state and local government agencies. For jobs in private businesses you may be asked to fill out other appropriate forms. You may also be asked to complete a skills test.

You can locate your nearest state employment agency by looking in the government office section in your telephone book. Services are provided to job seekers at no charge.

Private Agencies

Unlike state job agencies, private employment agencies charge fees for their services. These agencies receive job listings from employers and refer job seekers for specific positions. Often, an employer will ask the agency to refer only those people with certain skills or qualifications. The available position may require special training, a specific educational background, or other technical skills. The agency may ask to test you to determine what skills you have. Make sure you understand the purpose of the test, how it will help you, and if there is an extra fee involved.

Employment agencies need to charge fees in order to stay in business. A fee will be collected if the agency helps you get hired. The fee is usually based on a percentage of your salary. Sometimes the employer will pay the agency fee, but you should not count on it. Before you take a position, you should always know whether you or the employer will be responsible for the fee. Before you register with an agency, be sure you understand all financial arrangements.

If you are looking for a full-time job, an employment agency may be helpful. If you are looking for part-time employment or summer work while you are still in school, private agencies may not handle the kinds of jobs you are seeking.

Private Counselors

In addition to **counselors** who work for state or private agencies, there are private employment counselors who offer advice to job seekers. Unlike employment agencies, an independent counselor does not receive fees from employers. This kind of counselor concentrates on the individual job seeker and is paid by the applicant.

A private counselor can provide many services to job seekers. These may include assistance in choosing a career, writing resumes and letters, and giving advice about appearance, grooming, and interview behavior. Fees for these services vary. Charges may be determined by the amount of assistance required. Or a flat fee may be charged for a particular service such as resume preparation.

Be a careful consumer. Before you commit yourself to working with an employment counselor, be sure you understand how the counselor can help you, what services will be provided, and what they will cost. Don't buy more than you need, and be sure you need the services you buy. Remember that you're the one who has to look good to an employer in order to get the job. No one else can do that for you.

Temporary Job Agencies

Sometimes employers need someone to fill in for a regular employee or to help with a special project or an overload of work. These employers often rely on an agency that specializes in short-term employment. Work assignments may be for a single day, a week, a month, or even longer.

As with other employment agencies, you will be expected to complete application forms and perhaps be tested to determine your skill level. For example, clerical tests may be given to determine typing, filing, and word processing skills. The agency will match your skills with those requested by the employer needing temporary help. For people with good skills but little experience, temporary work can be an excellent way to learn about a variety of jobs. It is also a good way to establish a work record, and it can even lead to offers of permanent employment.

Usually you will be paid by the temporary agency rather than by the employer. Agencies charge the employer a fee for supplying temporary help. They do not collect fees from temporary workers.

School or College
Counseling/Placement Offices

If you are a student, your school or college may be able to help you find work—either part-time, full-time, or a summer job. High school counselors are sometimes contacted by employers in the community to post an available job or even to obtain a list of students seeking employment. Check with your counselors for information about possible assistance. Tell your counselors that you are looking for work and that you would appreciate any help they could give you.

While you are a student in a trade school or college there may be a number of offices that post information for both on-campus and off-campus job opportunities. Check with your college placement and financial aid offices. Also check for job notices in the student union and on bulletin boards in campus buildings. Tell your instructors, your dorm counselors, and your advisor that you are looking for a job. They may know of jobs, or they may be able to refer you to the appropriate offices.

As you near completion of your studies and begin to think about finding permanent employment, you will want to take advantage of your school or college's placement service. These offices may have direct job leads and can put you in touch with employers. Placement offices often arrange interview opportunities with employers who visit the school. Placement counselors can provide helpful information and assistance in all areas of a job search.

Personnel Departments

All large businesses have personnel departments. These departments handle questions about employment possibilities, collect application forms, and arrange interviews. Most often, your first contact with a company will be with the personnel department. Your application form and resume will be reviewed by a personnel specialist who may also conduct a screening interview. If you get past the screening interview, a second interview may be scheduled with the supervisor of the department that has the job opening.

The best way to obtain application materials and job information is to visit the personnel office. Calling to inquire about job openings is certainly appropriate, but always take the time to go in person as well. Large companies generally have jobs available throughout the year because of promotions, retirements, or resignations. For this reason, it is better to have an application on file rather than to rely only on calling to inquire about current openings.

Your first trip to a personnel office might only be to obtain an application form. Even though this visit may be brief, it is still important to look good. Prepare for it as carefully as you would for a scheduled interview. Dress appropriately, and take with you copies of your resume and any other materials you would normally take to an interview. It is better to have them and not use them than to be unprepared.

Personal Contacts

Telling people that you are looking for a job is sometimes the most effective way of finding one. Don't keep your plans a secret. Tell your neighbors, friends, and acquaintances. They know other people who might know about jobs, or they may even need to hire somebody for their own business.

Using personal contacts in this way is sometimes called *networking*. Understanding how a network operates is important. You are not asking for a job, but you are asking for job leads. Creating a network increases your chances of finding a job. The larger your network, the more opportunities you have for finding out about jobs. Building a network takes time—it doesn't happen overnight.

Most people will be willing to help you if you tell them what you want. People enjoy helping others, especially if they are not asked to go out of their way. Always be polite and remember to keep your contacts informed. Follow up on leads your contacts give you, and report back to them about what you have learned. Always show appreciation for their efforts either by a personal thank-you or by sending a note.

Combining Your Resources

The more you know about the way people find work, the better you are going to be at finding your own job. Talk to people and find out what's available in your community. Then use the resource or combination of resources that can help you the most.

As a high school student, Sarah Stebbens found her first job as a waitress by noticing a help wanted sign in a restaurant's window. During two years of part-time work she learned to meet people easily, to work under pressure, and to manage her time and money. When she needed a full-time job, she asked her fellow workers if they knew of any job leads. She also consulted her local public employment agency. There she took a civil service examination so she could apply for jobs with local and state government agencies. Soon after, she found a job as a clerk in the County Treasurer's office.

There she had the chance to develop her clerical skills and to continue to work with the public.

Now after a year, Sarah has moved to a larger city. She realizes that in a new community she doesn't have a network of friends and fellow workers to help her find a job. But she feels confident in her ability to present herself, to take advantage of her past experience, and to provide excellent references regarding her work performance. Sarah also knows that in addition to the sources of job information she has already used, she can consult newspaper ads, personnel departments, and private employment agencies.

Any one source of job information can be important in helping you find the job you want. More than likely you will use more than one of these sources during your first job search, and you may use most of them at some point in your working life.

Congratulations—You're Hired

Getting hired is an accomplishment you can take pride in. And starting a new job is always exciting. The same techniques you used to make employers want to hire you will help you look even better once you're on the job. Always be prepared and be on time. Ask intelligent questions and listen carefully to supervisors and coworkers. Have confidence in yourself and your abilities. Remember, you were hired because you were the best qualified person for the job.

The things you've learned in this book will continue to be useful to you in the years ahead. For many people, no matter how often they've looked for a job, starting a new job search always causes some worry. Learning to make yourself look good to employers can take much of the worry out of searching for a job. Following the guidelines in this book can help every job seeker attain his or her goal—getting hired for an interesting and rewarding position.

Steps to Looking Good

Step One: Identifying and understanding your needs, your interests, your skills and attributes, and making a commitment to your job search.

Step Two: Knowing how to prepare a resume and understanding how to use it.

Step Three: Communicating with employers by providing information on application forms and by writing purposeful letters.

Step Four: Taking the time to prepare for interviews, knowing how to conduct yourself at interviews, and following through after interviews.

Step Five: Overcoming obstacles to finding a job by seeing beyond the problem, dealing with the problem honestly, and maintaining a positive attitude.

Step Six: *Identifying possible employers, understanding how jobs are advertised, and knowing how to use available resources to learn about job possibilities.*

Chapter Review

Job Sources

How do employers advertise jobs? Do they use more than one method? Will the type of job I'm looking for determine the sources I can use?

Newspaper Ads

When do most ads appear? Which classifications will likely list the kind of job I'm seeking? How are words that apply to my skills and objectives commonly abbreviated?

Employment Services and Agencies

How can state employment services help me? What kind of employers list jobs with them? What is the difference between these public employment agencies and private agencies? What kinds of services does a private counselor provide? How do temporary job services assist employers? How can they help me?

Counseling/Placement Offices

How can my high school counselor help me find a job? What college offices can help me locate part-time or summer jobs? What services can help me find full-time work when I graduate?

Personnel Departments

What is the purpose of a personnel department? Why is it important to visit the personnel office? How can I make a good impression?

Personal Contacts

What is networking? How can it help me find a job?

Glossary

applicant *(page 1)* A person who applies for a job.

application form *(page 15)* A form that companies give job seekers to write down information about themselves.

benefits *(page 4)* Various things an employer offers to workers in addition to wages. Vacation time, medical insurance, and retirement plans are examples of benefits.

bonuses *(page 4)* Things that are given in addition to what is usual or expected.

commissions *(page 4)* Fees paid for work done based on a percentage of the total amount of business conducted.

commitment *(page 3)* A pledge made to do something; to be responsible for doing it.

compensation *(page 4)* The total payment and benefits given to employees in exchange for their work.

counselors *(page 99)* People whose job it is to give advice in a certain field, like education or finances.

dependents *(page 17)* People who rely on someone else for financial support.

disability *(page 4)* The lack of ability to perform tasks because of an injury, illness, or birth defect.

discrimination *(page 65)* Unfair treatment because of something such as your race, age, or sex.

documents *(page 5)* Written or printed papers that provide evidence, proof, or information about a particular object or subject.

employers *(page 1)* People or companies that hire workers.

employment *(page 1)* Work for pay.

essential *(page 4)* The most important or necessary thing.

evaluate *(page 63)* To determine the importance or worth of something by careful study.

graphics *(page 18)* Design elements, which might include drawings or photographs.

handicap *(page 79)* A condition that places a person at a disadvantage.

impairment *(page 85)* A damaged or weakened condition.

income *(page 6)* Payment in money for earnings from work, services, or investments.

interview *(page 55)* A meeting at which people ask questions of one another to gain information.

obstacles *(page 79)* Circumstances that may stand in your way and block your progress.

parole *(page 88)* The conditional release of a prisoner before his sentence has been completed.

peer pressure *(page 80)* The force or influence a group of people have over someone in their own group.

potential *(page 4)* Capability of further development.

probation *(page 87)* Allowing a person convicted of a minor crime to go free while being closely watched, and on the condition that all future behavior will be within the law.

promotion *(page 4)* A move to a better job with more pay.

qualified *(page 16)* Having the necessary abilities to perform a job.

recreation *(page 4)* Activity done for pleasure or relaxation.

references *(page 6)* People who can tell an employer whether someone can be a good worker.

research *(page 59)* To make a study or investigation of.

resources *(page 94)* Things that people can draw on for aid, support, or information.

responsibilities *(page 3)* Obligations that are either taken on or assigned.

resume *(page 1)* A short written history of a person's employment, education, and qualifications for a job.

retirement *(page 4)* When people stop working because of old age, poor health, or because they no longer need to earn money.

salary *(page 4)* Money an employer agrees to pay employees for their work.

Social Security card *(page 5)* An identification card that the United States government issues to people. The number on this card must be used on job application forms, tax forms, and other important records.

standard hourly minimum wage *(page 4)* The lowest pay rate that employers are allowed by law to pay full-time workers.

supervisors *(page 61)* Workers who are in charge of other workers and tell them what to do.

About the Authors

Rebecca Anthony and Gerald Roe are career specialists in the Educational Placement Office at The University of Iowa. They are the coauthors of *Finding a Job in Your Field, Educators' Passport to International Jobs,* and *From Contact to Contract: A Teacher's Employment Guide.* They began their careers as teachers in secondary schools.

Other Books of Interest

Careers: Exploration and Decision, Jack L. Rettig. Belmont, California: Fearon Education, David S. Lake Publishers, 1986.

Covers career selection and the process of career planning; explains why and how people choose careers; identifies occupational resources and discusses occupational trends.

Choices and Changes: A Career Book for Men, Joyce Slayton Mitchell. New York, New York: College Board Publications, 1982.

Covers career decisions and describes approximately one hundred different careers in the arts, business, communications, education, government, health sciences, social services, social sciences, and transportation.

I Can Be Anything: A Career Book for Women, Joyce Slayton Mitchell. New York, New York: College Board Publications, 1982.

Covers career descriptions for women of all ages; discusses topics such as changing job opportunities, the earning gap between the sexes, and the importance of achieving economic independence.

Job Hunting for the Disabled, Edith Marks and Adele Lewis. Woodbury, New Jersey: Barron's Educational Series, Inc., 1983.

Covers job search preparation and strategies for the handicapped; discusses legislation and rights of handicapped workers and gives job tips and information about training programs.

Jobs for Teenagers, Ilene Jones, New York, New York: Ballantine Books, 1983.

Covers a variety of topics including job connections, places likely to hire teenagers, budgets, taxes, managing money, self-employment, working with kids, and summer job opportunities.

Summer Employment Directory. Cincinnati, Ohio: Writer's Digest Books

Covers 50,000 summer jobs at resorts, hotels, camps, national parks, ranches, restaurants, conference and training centers, businesses, and with the government; revised annually.

Index

Abbreviations, in classified ads, 95–97
Action phrases, in resume, 19–20
Action words, in resume 19
Agencies, employment (*see* Employment agencies)
Application form, 37–42
    as screening device, 37–38
    preparation of, 37–38
    purpose of, 37–38
    samples, 39–42
Application, letter of, 46–49
    purpose of, 46
    samples, 47–49
Attributes, 8–10

Bonuses, 4
Business letters, 43–52, 69–73
    application letter, 46–49
    folding of, 50–51
    follow-up letter, 69–73
    parts of, 43
    styles, 44–45

Certificates, 5–6
Classified ads, 46, 94–97
    abbreviations in, 95–97
    categories, 94
Clothing, 5, 56
    for interviews, 56
    work, 5
Commissions, 4
Commitment, 11

Compensation, 4
Counselors, employment, 99–101
    private, 99–100
    school, 101
Criminal record, 87–89

Discrimination, 64–65
Dictionary of Occupational Titles, 7
Disability (*see* Handicap)
Documents, personal, 5–6
    certificates, 5–6
    licenses, 5–6
    Social Security card, 5
Dropout, school, 80–82

Employment agencies, 98–100
    private, 99
    private counselors, 99–100
    public, 98
    temporary, 100
Envelopes, 50
    addressing of, 50
    sizes, 50

Fired, 82–84

General Education Development (GED), 80

Handicap, 84–87
Help wanted, 46, 98
    ads, 46
    signs, 98

Impairment (*see* Handicap)
Income, 4, 66
    asking about, 66
    benefits, 4
    salary, 4
Interests, 7
Interview, 55–74
    behavior, 60–62
    clothing, 56
    don'ts, 61–62
    dos, 59–60
    ending, 66–67
    evaluation, 69
    follow-up letters, 69–73
    grooming, 55–56
    image, 55
    materials, 57–58
    preparation, 58–59
    questions, applicant, 65–66
    questions, employer, 63–65
    questions, inappropriate,
        64–65
    records, 67–69
    research, 58–59
    unscheduled, 62

Job offers, 74–75
Job satisfaction, 6–7
Job sources, 93–104
    classified ads, 94–97
    employment agencies, 98–100
    help wanted signs, 98
    personal contacts, 102–103
    personnel departments,
        101–102
    placement offices, 101
    school counselors, 101

Letters (*see* Business letters)
Licenses, 5–6

Minimum wage, 4

Needs, 3–6
    clothing, 5
    income, 4
    personal documents, 5–6
    references, 6
    schedule, 3–4
    transportation, 5
Networking, 101–103
Newspaper ads, 46, 48–49, 94–97
    abbreviations in, 95–97

Obstacles, employment, 79–89
    attitude, 79–80, 89
    criminal record, 87–89
    dropout, 80–82
    fired, 82–84
    handicap, 84–87

Parole, 88
Personnel departments, 101–102
Placement office, 101
Private employment agencies, 99
Probation, 87–88
Public employment agencies, 98

Records, interview, 67–69
    samples, 68
References, 6
    telephone, 6
Rejection, 11–12, 89
Research, 58–59
    company information, 58–59
Resume, 15–34
    action phrases in, 19–20
    action words in, 19
    definition, 15
    headings, 20–21

interviewing, 16, 57
irrelevant information, 17
production of, 18, 34
rules, 17-19
samples, 23-33
updating, 34
use of, 15-16

Salary, 4, 66
   asking about, 66
Schedule, 3-4
   full-time work, 3
   part-time work, 3
Skills, 8-9, 57-58, 98-100
   illustrations of, 57-58
   testing, 98-100
Social Security card, 5, 57

Temporary job agencies, 100
Tests, pre-employment, 85, 98-100
   chemical dependency, 85
   skills, 98-100
Transportation, 5

Uniforms, work, 5, 56

ZIP Code, 50